NORMAN MEIER

SALES
LEADERSHIP

HOW TO BUILD AND LEAD A SALES ORGANIZATION

Norman Meier

authorHOUSE®

AuthorHouse™
1663 Liberty Drive
Bloomington, IN 47403
www.authorhouse.com
Phone: 1 (800) 839-8640

Published by AuthorHouse 08/11/2016

ISBN: 978-1-5049-7816-3 (sc)
ISBN: 978-1-5049-7815-6 (e)

Print information available on the last page.

Any people depicted in stock imagery provided by Thinkstock are models, and such images are being used for illustrative purposes only. Certain stock imagery © Thinkstock.

This book is printed on acid-free paper.

Dedication

This book is dedicated to my friend and designer Mariano Duyos. Mariano has been working with me for a few years now and he has designed the entire collection of NM International products. His skills and taste are simply impeccable.

I could not have started and completed my programs without his help. He has helped me to live my own dream and for that I am eternally grateful.

Out of all the programs that Mariano designed he became a "fan" of the leadership series. That is why I solely dedicate this book to him.

Thank you for everything that you have done. You are truly amazing.

Norman

Foreword

What does it mean to be a good sales leader? It means that you have to produce great results. A leader has to lead employees. Your employees are the most important part of your company – no matter what your company does. Besides operating your business, you need an additional set of skills to be successful as an entrepreneur or as a manager. These skills are leadership skills and they are completely different than the other skills. One of the key components of being able to grow a company is for you to lead your employees effectively.

LEADERS ARE NOT BORN - THEY ARE MADE

Just as there are laws of nature that cannot be changed and always stay the same; there are laws of business success. I have built and managed several businesses in my career. I have started many new companies and financed them with millions of dollars and I took several companies public in the stock market. One of those companies was valued at over $300 million. I have started many international companies and traveled the world doing business. I have built organizations in Europe and North America. Making the right strategic decisions to have a successful business is key. But it is the way that you must think and act that will set you apart from the rest of the crowd.

LEADERSHIP CANOT REALLY BE TAUGHT. IT CAN ONLY BE LEARNED

Being a great leader really means to build the right team. Without the right people a company or organization is nothing. You cannot be a great leader on your own. Finding the right people and getting them to perform on a high level is a challenging task. People and personalities are so different and it is a difficult job to get them to work in harmony and work towards a common goal. The goal of this book is to identify the steps necessary to build a successful team. Like in every sports team, for example, you will need stars, people who are the backbone and perform consistently and new people who need to be developed.

In the following program you will learn some of the lessons that I have learned from building and running several sales teams and organizations.

PEOPLE OFTEN SAY THAT MOTIVATION DOESN'T LAST

Well, neither does bathing - that's why it is recommend daily. Motivation of your employees is a key ingredient when it comes to building a successful organization. In order to achieve greater results, you must know and understand how to motivate your people. The same things don't motivate everyone and it is important to apply a variety of tools and techniques to get your employees to perform better. It is your job as a leader to motivate the whole team and to find out what motivates and drives each employee individually. If you can create a motivating work environment for your employees, they will be happier and perform better, which is good for you. If you fail to motivate your people, it will eventually create a negative environment and the end of the organization won't be too far. I have put together a variety to ideas and tools that I have used in the past. I have also learned and understood what drives people and how important and essential the right kind of motivation can be.

WHY AM I QUALIFIED TO TALK ABOUT THIS SUBJECT?

In my entire career I managed many employees and sales people. I started out in the biggest independent financial planning sales organization in Europe and worked my way up the ladder. In 1997 I was the number one team leader with the best sales result of my team. I competed against 1000 other team leaders in Europe and created a new sales record. I was promoted to sales manager and became one the top leaders in that organization. I trained and managed around 75 sales people during that time and I was only 23 years old back then. When I went into the hedge fund industry I became the global sales manager for the biggest independent hedge fund company in the world. I managed a team of very bright and sometimes-arrogant young people with impressive University degrees and we improved the overall sales team result from $42 million in a four month period to over $245 million just one year later. Then later on I built my own sales teams and organization when I went into the Private Equity field and I managed over 60 people. My team and I raised over $40 million in only two years from 500 investors. During my entire career I hired, fired, motivated, encouraged, trained, led, promoted, evaluated and educated a lot of new sales people and employees. This program is a summary of my personal leadership experience. This knowledge is real and comes from actual experience from the business world. Leadership, a critical management skill, is the ability to motivate a group of people toward a common goal.

CONTENTS

CHAPTER 1: LEADERSHIP SKILLS

CHAPTER 2: STRATEGIC LEADERSHIP AND BUSINESS SUCCESS

CHAPTER 3: BUILDING A SUCCESSFUL TEAM

CHAPTER 4: MOTIVATION FOR YOUR EMPLOYEES

CHAPTER 5: BECOMING A GREAT SALES MANAGER AND LEADER

ANNEX

LEADERSHIP
SKILLS

Introduction

A leader has to lead employees. Your employees are the most important part of your company – no matter what your company does.

Besides operating your business, you need an additional set of skills to be successful as an entrepreneur or as a manager. These skills are leadership skills and they are completely different than the other skills. It is not enough to know how to operate your business or how to sell products to your clients or how to manage and operate your business operations. One of the key components of being able to grow a company is for you to lead your employees effectively.

> **If your leadership is weak, your company is weak and everything can fall apart.**

Therefore, I have put together the most important leadership skills from my point of view that should help you to become a more effective leader and manager.

Why am I qualified to talk about this subject?

I have started, built and run many companies during my career. I have employed many employees and I have seen the good, the bad and the ugly. I have had successful companies and successful leadership and I have had companies that turned into a complete disaster because of mistakes in my leadership style. I have learned what works well and what is not ideal.

I have had 75 employees when I was in my twenties working for a financial planning organization and over 100 employees when I was in my early thirties working for my own companies. I have had to deal with sales people, technical people, administrational staff, external consultants, managers, specialists with PhDs and regular staff.

I believe that I did a great job with most people but I also learned from mistakes and what not to do when things get difficult. I would like to share my personal knowledge and experience with you and I hope that it will help you to become a more successful leader.

Stay positive in every situation

Business life is not a very smooth path. Things always go wrong and you will always be faced with all kinds of problems. If you accept this as a normal part of business, you will be a lot less stressed and you can deal more effectively with every difficult situation.

> *Always ask the question: What is most important right now?*

The key is not to lose your cool but to focus on what is most important in any given situation. If there are 10 fires burning at the same time, you can only focus on one at a time. It is easy to lose your head and patience when things get ugly. So the most important factor in difficult situations is to stay positive.

When things are on fire and go wrong, you should know that this is not a permanent situation and that it will pass. Calmer times will always follow. So don't lose your temper and stay positive. Being positive will help you to get through those times. Always expect a positive outcome in the end.

Be available

Don't avoid problems or people when things go wrong. You need to face difficult situations as soon as possible even if it is difficult. When things are bad, you need to be available in the office and in person. You need to show up and be available. You cannot try to fix things over the phone or by email. If things go really bad, there is no substitute for showing up.

> *There is almost nothing worse that you can do in a difficult situation than to hide or turn off communications. In a moment like this you can either come out stronger and with more respect as a leader or lose everything.*

You cannot expect your employees to fix the situation or a conflict on their own. That is why you are the manager. You need to make the difficult decisions even if they are unpopular but in the best interest of the organization.

Have clear and strong values

In order to always know what to do in any given situation, you need to have clear and strong values that you have defined in the beginning. Those are your rules.

You should set goals for the organization and develop a strategic plan for its achievement. You should set milestones and define what your organization's values are. Especially when things get difficult, you need to have a clear head and know what to do.

> *If you have clear values for things that you stand for and things that you will not stand for, then there is no question or doubt what needs to be done.*

Do you stand for customer service and quality or do you want sales results at any cost? Do you accept an internal conflict in your organization that could rip the team apart or are you ready to fire key people even though it might hurt your bottom line? Are you willing to follow through on your ideals even though you might lose popularity within your organization?

Show heart

In general, it is better to be on the stricter side than to be too soft with your employees. But that doesn't mean that you have no heart. Especially, when someone gets sick or there is a problem in the family, you must act with your heart.

> *If you show heart in the right situation,*
> *you will have the loyalty of your employee forever.*

That also means that you don't always strictly follow the rules and make exceptions. There are situations and people that deserve a different treatment and you don't need to stubbornly follow every rule. There are situations that are really though for certain people and if you make the wrong decision and stick with your rules, you will lose the employee sooner or later. If your employee is important to the organization it is ok to treat him or her differently.

> *You don't need to treat everybody the same and with*
> *the same rules. That is a myth. True leaders recognize when*
> *they need to make an exception.*

Never show any doubt

The price that you pay for being a leader is often that you are alone with your problems and worries. It is normal to have doubts and not to know everything.

> *You can never share your doubts with your employees.*
> *No one will follow a leader who has doubts.*

If you have doubts and you need to talk about them, then talk to your friends, other business colleagues who are on the same level like you or your superiors (if you have any). Talk to your wife or husband or even your dog (ha, ha...) but **NEVER EVER** talk to your employees about it.

> **Doubt is like a virus that will spread.**

It will go into the heads of your employees and will lead to the fall of your organization.

Have clear rules and communicate your expectations in the beginning

In every organization there are a number of internal rules and ways to behave that need to be followed. It is often much harder and frustrating for you to constantly criticize a new employee and tell him what he has done wrong. This will lower his motivation and you constantly get upset because he is not behaving in the manner that you would like.

It is much better to communicate your rules and expectations in the beginning when someone joins your organization. You let them know exactly what you expect and what kind of behavior is unacceptable. Once you have done this, it will be much easier for you to lead.

I would also recommend having a written employee manual where those rules are explained and even have the new employee sign this document. This way, you have clearly communicated and in case you need to get rid of someone who is not following your rules or fulfilling your expectations, you can refer to the employee manual.

Have a clear vision

Each organization needs to have a mission statement. This is a vision of how the organization should ideally be in the future. But you can also have a vision for your team within the organization. The more you communicate and live your vision, the more your employees will accept it.

A great vision will be a big motivator for everyone and people will identify themselves more with your organization. A vision is a good indicator if you are on the right path and it will help every employee to make the right decisions, too.

> *Communicate your vision regularly with your team.*
> *The more people believe in the same goal,*
> *the more likely it will become a reality.*

Every time someone is doing something that is not in alignment with that vision, your employees will tell other employees to correct their behavior.

Set goals for each employee

Each employee is different and motivated by different things. As a leader it is your job to recognize the different personalities. It is important for you to develop a personal relationship with each employee and have private one-on-one talks on a regular basis. In those personal talks you need to find out what makes your employee tick and what his goals are. The more you can help him to achieve his goals, the better will he perform.

You should also find out what kind of strengths or interests your employee has and see if there is a way to include them in the organization. People who are live out their talents will do much better because they are in the right place.

> **Develop a personal goal plan for each employee and talk about it in each personal meeting.**

You should make a connection between his activities from his sales efforts and his personal goals. Encourage and motivate him to reach his personal goals by performing better at his job and therefore making for money.

Training and education can be more important than motivation

Every new employee has to learn new things. At first, it is normal that the job will be done poorly since the new job and its responsibilities need to be learned first.

A lot of managers make the mistake that they teach them quickly a few things in the beginning and then leave them on their own. They fail to continue to teach them the necessary skills and knowledge and only use motivation to try to get better results out of them.

In my experience you need to make sure that you help your employee by doing more trainings and improve his skills by teaching him things rather than just giving motivation.

> **Motivation is important but it will not help someone to get better. New employees need to be enabled to perform better.**

This is especially true for new sales people. You need to practice with them and do role-play. You need to find out where they are weak so that you can give them the skills they need to become better.

If you have the choice between motivating someone or helping them with a training, you should always use the time to teach them something.

Include your team in a major decision

> *You have two choices when it comes to big decisions:*
> *You can either communicate what the new decision is*
> *or you can ask your people for their opinion.*

Some things cannot be changed and there is no room for a discussion. But the team can influence some decisions. In general, it is much better if the team supports a decision because then everyone will accept it. You can have a team meeting and explain the circumstances of your situation and come logically to the conclusion what the new decision for the team should be. Then you can ask for their opinions and get feedback.

Remember, you are never as smart as an entire team. Together, there can be better or more ideal solutions to a problem. But if you include your people in a decision, they will be more open to accept it.

Criticism can be a killer to your people's motivation

> *Just because you have the title "boss"*
> *doesn't mean that you have the title "jerk".*

If you are a jerk and criticize people constantly, you will not get the desired results out of them.

If you feel that you must dominate someone by putting them down, then you are in the wrong position or you have a personality problem. **Criticism or feedback is necessary BUT it is crucial HOW it is done.**

Here are some rules:

1. Never criticize someone in front of other people.

Criticism should only be done in private between you and your employee. Nothing can embarrass or destroy someone's self-worth more than being criticized in front of a group.

2. If you criticize someone you should only criticize THE BEHAVIOR and NEVER THE PERSON.

Don't say: *"You are a real idiot because you did that..."* Instead you should say that they action or behavior was unacceptable and never attack the person itself.

3. Every criticism needs to be followed by a positive compliment and encouragement of better behavior.

You could say: *"Your behavior was unacceptable. I expect more of a person of your caliber and personality. This is not typical for your standards. Normally, you are such a great person."*

4. Always ask yourself what the goal of your criticism is.

Do you really want to correct a behavior or do you want to show who is in charge because you feel that your authority has been challenged? Remember: You can win an argument but you can lose the person.

5. People should respect you but not fear you.

You should choose your battles and not constantly put someone down if they have done something wrong. If you create an environment of fear, you will have a very bad morale in your organization, which will eventually lead to its end.

Lead by example

> *Following by example is extremely powerful.*

If you're in sales, you should show your people that you could produce more sales than anyone. Besides all your responsibilities as a manager you should show them that you could produce a substantial amount of sales. You should either have a track record from the past where you were the best in the organization and you should have proof of that or you show them every day how they should perform by doing some sales yourself.

Don't expect people to do things if you haven't done them yourself. You don't even need any kind of leadership skills or motivational speeches if you show them how it is done on a regular basis. People will listen to your advice if they know that you are doing what they are supposed to be doing. If you don't lead by example, you will eventually lose respect and authority.

Become an outstanding manager

> *Respect is earned – not automatically given*

Just because you are the manager and boss doesn't mean that you automatically have the respect of your people. You need to earn the respect first. Everything that you do will either give you more respect or less.

The manner and the way that you behave and communicate is key. If you say something, you must do it and follow through. You need to show your people that you are doing the best in your area and you need to show them how your efforts have a direct impact on the results and development of the organization.

You need to be absolutely professional, honest and with the highest amount of integrity. Always tell the truth, show strength and character in every situation. Do things for your people that improve their working conditions so that it helps them to perform better. Stand up for your employees and show them that you are in the same court as them.

In everything that you do you should be as professional as possible. Set high standards for yourself and you will see that people will try to follow you by setting higher standards themselves. Always tell the truth and keep your promises. It is better to face problems with the truth and communicate them instead of trying to hide them. Sooner or later the truth will always come out and the result will be worse.

Be results oriented – not task oriented

> **In the end all that counts are results.**

It doesn't matter how you got there or how nicely you executed it. Show your people that you honor results and that it doesn't matter how well their binders in the office are labeled. The only thing that matters is results, sales and profits. Everything else is irrelevant.

You are in a business to make a profit and to get customers. Everything that you do in the office should be focused on helping that goal.

There are certain people that are very focused on the tasks and on trying to make things perfect or the right way. Those kinds of people are important when it comes to areas like product development or other areas.

But **if you are in a sales organization, task-oriented people are in the wrong place**. Task-oriented people lose too much time on trying to execute a certain job and in the end they don't get the job finished on time.

Get people to perform better because of you

Your job as a manager is to develop an emotional connection with your people.

> *People should want to reach their results because of you*
> *and because they don't want to disappoint you.*

It should be irrelevant what the company does or what your superiors expect. It is important that the employee wants to perform well for you and doesn't want to let you down.

I personally have made the experience that you need to develop a close relationship with your people. There are certain boundaries that need to be in place like money, your personal family, etc. But in general I have learned that you will get better access to your people if you don't act like "the boss" and more like a friend.

Just because you have a personal and close relationship with your employee doesn't mean that he doesn't give you the respect that you deserve. It is a matter of personality and character of the employee.

You should know how far you can go with certain people and where you need to draw the line. In general, don't go out to a bar or clubs with your people. Don't do any inappropriate things that could lessen your level of respect. Private activities should stay out of the office environment. But having a close and personal relationship is important so that you can steer and influence your employee in the right direction in case he is getting off track.

Respect is always a two-way street. So if you are respectful in every situation with your people, they will be respectful in return. People who cross that line cannot stay in the organization.

The employee wants to reach his sales goals because you made a pact or agreement with him. You help and support him and in return you expect him to do his job exceptionally well.

But make sure that you are not being too friendly all the time. Even though most of us want to be seen as friendly and approachable to people in our team. After all, people are happier working for a manager that they get along with.

However, you'll sometimes have to make tough decisions regarding people in your team, and some people will be tempted to take advantage of your relationship if you're too friendly with them. This doesn't mean that you can't socialize with your people. But, you do need to get the balance right between being a friend and being the boss and set clear boundaries.

Always give lots of praise and recognition

> *People are starving for love and attention.*
> *They need praise and recognition like they need air to survive.*

If you create a working environment where employees are valued and are given recognition, they will strive to perform better. **People get way too little recognition in their personal lives.** You want to create an environment where people like to come to work and where they feel appreciated and valued.

The more positive the environment and general mood is the better will be the overall performance. **Therefore you should give out praise and recognition as much as possible.**

Often, managers make the mistake that they don't say anything if someone is doing something well and only say something if they are doing something wrong. In rare exception they give out moderate praise if someone has done something exceptionally well.

But this is a very frustrating environment for an employee and eventually most people will pursue other careers or jobs where they feel that they are properly valued and appreciated.

You cannot give out too much praise. Try to catch them when they are doing something good and try to give praise in front of other people.

Remember the rule:

> *Criticism can never be given in front of other people*
> *but praise should be given in front of other people if possible.*

Have daily contact

As a manager and leader **you should always know where your people stand with their results and activities.** If you are trying to reach a monthly sales goal and you start asking questions after 2 weeks, you have no more time to influence activities and to reach your goal. The result is up to chance and luck.

A good manager always knows how many meetings and open potential their people have. That is why you should have daily contact. You should always ask about their activities so that you have a good idea what needs to be done and you can influence someone's behavior in time.

The other factor why daily contact is so important is because **you need to know where your employee stands emotionally.**

Especially in sales, the emotional state of your employee is key for this result. Do you know what is going on in his private life? Could this be a factor why he not performing well? Does he still believe in the company and its products? Is he still emotionally on board with the company?

> *As a manager you should always know how*
> *your people feel and where they are at emotionally.*
> *Some people will need special attention or motivation.*

Common leadership and management mistakes

Failing to provide feedback is the most common mistake that leaders make. When you don't provide prompt feedback to your people, you're depriving them of the opportunity to improve their performance. If you catch someone doing something the wrong way, you must correct the behavior immediately and not wait until your weekly meeting.

A lot of managers also misunderstand what really motivates their people. It is not just money that drives them. Many leaders make the mistake of assuming that their team is only working for monetary reward.

However, it's unlikely that this will be the only thing that motivates them. Some people are seeking a greater work/life balance, appreciate the flexibility of how the work can be done, and others will be motivated by factors such as achievement, extra responsibility, praise, or a sense of camaraderie. Another common mistake is that some managers believe that they are the only ones who can do the job the right way. They take on too much work and never delegate anything.

> *Make sure that you don't become the slave of the organization. You need to delegate.*

And then there are people who delegate jobs but then don't follow up properly to check whether it has been done correctly.

You can't delegate everything

Delegation is an important factor when it comes to managing people. But some managers are being too "hands-off" instead of "hands-on". Many managers want to avoid micromanaging their people. But going to the opposite extreme (with a hand-offs management style) isn't a good idea either. You need to get the balance right in order to get things done.

> *Some people are simply not making enough time*
> *for their people. It is understandable when you're a manager,*
> *that it's easy to get so wrapped up in your own workload*
> *that you don't make yourself available to your team.*

Yes, you have projects that you need to deliver. But your people must come first. Without you being available when they need you, your people won't know what to do, and they won't have the support and guidance that they need to meet their objectives.

You can avoid this by blocking out time in your schedule on a regular basis specifically for your people. Your door doesn't always have to be open because otherwise you don't get any work done yourself but in the end, your team should always come first.

This is what leadership is all about. So make sure that you allocate enough time to your people and let them know when you are available when you cannot be disturbed.

Don't expect things that you didn't do yourself

If you make personal telephone calls during work time, or speak negatively about your superiors, you must assume that your people will do the same. You cannot expect things from them and then do them yourself. **As a leader, you need to be a role model for your team.**

This means that if they need to stay late, you should also stay late to help them. Or, if your organization has a rule that no one eats at their desk, then set the example and head to the break room every day for lunch.

The same goes for your attitude. If you're negative some of the time, you can't expect your people not to be negative. So remember, your team is watching you all the time. **If you want to shape their behavior, start with your own.**

> **If you want people to work hard, you must be the first and last person in the office. Otherwise they won't do it.**

If you don't want people to speak badly about you, you should never speak badly about another employee or person yourself. Employees will always copy your behavior and that is why one of the best strategies is to lead by example in every situation.

Develop your emotional intelligence

> **The most important skill for a manager is to develop emotional intelligence.**

You can only change things for the better if you understand what drives your people and where things are going into the wrong direction. Managers who lack emotional intelligence and who are oblivious to what is happening around them, will lose key employees and will never really get ahead. By getting a sixth sense of what your team needs and then being able to identify it, you can change things for the better.

When the shit hits the fan (dealing with difficult situations)

> **Difficult times won't last forever – so keep your head up**

If you have clearly defined what your strategic plan is then you can easier deal with any crisis.

It is important that you show strength in difficult times and not weakness, doubt or dispair. You need to have clarity about the steps that need to be taken in order to get out of the mess. The cooler your behavior is, the better. If you are stressed out, your team will get stressed out and that doesn't help anybody.

You should not get emotional in situations like these because problems and crisis is a normal part of business life. The more clarity you have in regards to what your organizational goals and what your values are, the easier it will be for you to make the right decisions.

> *A crisis can also be a good thing.*
> *Sometimes it shows you what is wrong with your organization and what needs to be changed. Embrace a crisis and don't condemn it.*

When some things are falling out of place they might actually be falling into place.

Sometimes you needed to get rid of a certain employee or a supplier. By eliminating this factor, you might be much better off in the future.

CHAPTER 2

STRATEGIC
LEADERSHIP
AND BUSINESS SUCCESS

Introduction

> **Leaders are not born – they are made**

All successful people men and women are big dreamers. They imagine what their future could be, ideal in every respect, and then they work every day toward their distant vision, that goal or purpose. Having the right kind of focus is key for strategic development and the success of a business.

That is why a leader must have a vision. This vision must be communicated, lived and supported by everyone.

Dreams can become a reality when we possess a vision that is characterized by the willingness to work hard and a desire for excellence. A vision comes first and then a strategic and tactical plan for its achievement. **A vision requires courage and the ability to think big.**

Strategic leadership from personal experience

> **The principles of business success are always the same.
> Once you have built one successful business,
> you can build other successful businesses.**

Just as there are laws of nature that cannot be changed and always stay the same; **there are laws of business success.**

I have built and managed several businesses in my career. I have started many new companies and financed them with millions of dollars and I took several companies public in the stock market. One of those companies was valued at over $300 million.

I have started many international companies and traveled the world doing business. I have built organizations in Europe and North America. I have led many employees and one of my companies had more than 100 people all over the world.

Making the right strategic decisions to have a successful business is key. But it is the way that you must think and act that will set you apart from the rest of the crowd.

In this chapter I have put together **the most important lessons about strategic leadership.**

Develop a vision and big goals

> *Leadership is the capacity to translate vision into reality.*

Every business must have a vision. In order for you to determine what that vision is, you should answer the following questions:

Determine your REAL core business:

- What business are you in?
- What business are you really in?
- What business should you be in?
- What business could you be in?

Determine the values of your business:

- What does your company stand for?
- What does your company not stand for?
- What is the single most important objective of the company?
- What are your 3 most important personal values, business values and business goals?

When a plan or strategy fails, people are tempted to assume it was the wrong vision. **Plans and strategies can always be changed and improved. But a vision doesn't change. Visions are simply refined with time.**

There are people who are really good managers, people who can manage a big organization, and then there are people who are very analytic or focused on strategy. Those two types don't usually tend to be in the same person. The question is, in which category would you put yourself?

Vision is the art of seeing what is invisible to others. **Good leaders must communicate vision clearly, creatively, and continually.** However, the vision doesn't come alive until the leader models it.

> *Vision without action is merely a dream.*
> *Action without vision just passes the time.*
> *Vision with action can change the world.*

The one thing that you have that nobody else has is you. Your voice, your mind, your story, your vision. So write and draw and build and play and dance and live as only you can. People buy into the leader before they buy into the vision.

Don't let negativity or negative people affect your vision. A lot of people may say harsh things or ridicule you, but don't let it affect you. If anything, it should give you more enthusiasm and push you to do better in your career so that you can prove them wrong.

Failed plans should not be interpreted as a failed vision. Visions don't change, they are only refined. Plans rarely stay the same, and are scrapped or adjusted as needed. **Be stubborn about the vision, but flexible with your plan. You must continually tweak the plan the daily execution.**

A vision gets the dream started. Dreaming employs your God-given imagination to reinforce the vision. This is absolutely necessary to building the life of your dreams.

Planning a strategy for profitability

> *Your ability to do accurate costing for your products and services and to set proper prices can make all the difference between profits, losses, success and failure.*

The main reason why you are in business in the first place is to make money. In order to create a successful business enterprise you must be very clear about your products, pricing and profits. Having great products but not making enough money will lead to the failure of the company.

The key measure in business success is customer satisfaction. You must ask yourself how your products and services add value and how they contribute to the life of your customer.

The most important key activity for a successful business is SALES. How do you create sales for your company? What kind of marketing activities will support your selling process?

> *Sales is the business of converting leads into paying customers.*
> *Marketing is the process of lead generation.*
> *The purpose of a business is to create and keep a customer.*

You must develop a sales strategy and have clear written goals on how you are going to achieve it.

In marketing you must define the six P's. Those six P's are:

- Product or service
- Price
- Promotion
- Packaging
- Positioning
- People

What is your product or service exactly? What is the price you are selling your products for? How do you go about promotion, packaging and how do you position your products? Who are the people that you are targeting?

There are four keys to success in marketing:

- The first key to marketing is **specialization** in a particular product, service, market or customer. You can't be good at everything.

- The second key is **differentiation**. What is your competitive advantage? What makes you superior or better than the competition?

- The third key is **segmentation**: Determine exactly who your potential customers are.

- And the fourth is **concentration**: Where should you concentrate your time, money, efforts and resources to get the very best customers?

> *You must continually ask yourself the brutal questions about your business and its potential. If something doesn't work, you must have the courage to discontinue it.*

You must be very clear about everything. You must continually ask yourself why you are doing something in the first place. The goal is to create profits. **If an activity or product is not giving you the desired result, it is time to make some changes.**

Therefore, you must do test marketing first. You should get immediate results for your advertising: If they don't come right away, stop doing it.

Accept complete responsibility for your business life. Refuse from this day forward to make excuses or blame anyone or anything. You are in business to succeed and you must find out what works and what doesn't work.

The power of clarity

*Get the facts. **Get the REAL FACTS.** Not the hoped-for facts, the assumed facts, or the possible facts. Facts don't lie.*

Clarity is the most important thing. If you are not clear, nothing is going to happen. You have to be clear. Then you have to be confident about your vision. And after that, you just have to put a lot of work in.

In every industry, the top 20% of activities or products make the 80% of the profits.

You should know all the critical numbers in your business if you want to thrive.

What are your indirect costs? What are your direct costs when selling a product? Run your business like a turnaround business. Be thoughtful and careful about every expenditure. The better you know all your real numbers, the more able you make appropriate changes and improvements.

There is no substitution for clarity and being absolutely realistic when it comes to numbers. **Numbers don't lie.** They give you real insight in what needs to be done or changed – no matter what your people are saying. Therefore, you must be like a detective and **focus on the reality so that you can positively change the outcome.**

Develop and implement a successful marketing and sales strategy

When it comes to selling your product, you must ask the following questions:

Product:

- How can you convince a skeptical customer to buy from you?
- How do you produce, package, ship and deliver your product once you have sold it, to ensure high level of quality?
- How will you follow-up and service your customer to ensure a high level of satisfaction and repeat business?
- How can you continually increase your sales and profitability?
- How can you exceed customer expectations?

Identify your ideal customer:

- Who is your ideal customer?
- Why does your customer buy your product or service?
- What value or benefit does he or she seek or get from buying your product?
- What is your competitive advantage?
- Who is your competition and why do customers buy from them rather than from you?

Business success and growth questions:

- What business constraints or factors are holding your business success back? What slows you down?
- What 20% of the activities could account for 80% of your results?
- How could you become the very best company in your industry or field?
- What are the most important skills that you need to develop to move to the top 10% in your field?
- What are your major limiting factors and what can you do to remove those?
- What are the biggest problems or obstacles in your business or personal life? What are possible solutions?
- What would you want to be or do if you had absolutely no limitations and success was guaranteed?

You need to answer all of these questions first, in order to define your sales and marketing strategy. **Based on the answers, your strategy will differ.**

If you have an existing product right now, go through these questions again to see if you might find a better way of selling your products to customers.

Having the right people can make all the difference

> *"Teamwork makes the dream work, but a vision becomes a nightmare when the leader has a big dream and a bad team."*
> (John C. Maxwell)

You can't achieve success all by yourself. That is not possible.

You also need great people around you who help you achieve your vision. It is crucial for your success that you have the right team. But it **is almost impossible to achieve a great goal with the wrong people.**

The quality of your people is one of the most important factors in business success. You should try to hire the best people possible but you should also focus on developing your existing staff to become better. **Teach, train and develop your people.**

You can't expect people to perform at high levels until you have thoroughly trained them to perform at that level. **Take control of your team and its development.** Make sure that everyone is performing at his or her best.

As a leader, you should never forget that everyone needs encouragement. And everyone who receives it, young or old, successful or less-than-successful, unknown or famous, is changed by it. **We all need encouragement one way or another. As the leader it is your job to motivate your team.**

Strategic business development

> *Think on paper. Take the time to sit down*
> *and review the key numbers and data for your business.*

One of the best ways to determine whether you are on track with your goals is to take a pad of paper and a pen. Write down the forecast of each team member or group for the next six months.

Try to be as realistic with your forecast as possible. **Thinking on paper and writing down the overall numbers will help you to see what needs to be done.**

In the age of computers and the Internet it is often hard to see the forest for the trees. Sometimes it is much easier to just go outside for a couple of hours with a pen and paper and to draw up your business. It helps to recreate the plan on paper on a regular basis to see what your goals are and where you need to make changes.

Business growth

> *Law of nature: a life that is no longer growing – must die.*
> *The same law applies to the life of a business.*
> *If you are not growing, you should no longer exist.*

Your strategy must be aggressive. You cannot sit back and relax – ever! There is no point in running a business if you don't want to grow and expand. The focus must always be to growth-oriented. **You must continually ask yourself the question on how you can add products and services and improve the existing strategy.** 80% of all products and services will be obsolete in five years. The world is constantly changing and this is true more than ever.

Focus on achieving your vision and that big goal of yours. The interesting part of the Universe is that you can be, do or have anything that you want if you go out there and make it happen.

Building a sales-oriented organization

> *The key to business success is high sales;*
> *the reason for business failure is low sales;*
> *all else is commentary.*

Sales and marketing are the number one activities in your company. **Your product development is pointless if you have low sales.** Without sales, there is no business life.

A study has found out that **the number one reason for business success is high sales and the number one reason for business failure is low sales.** Everything else is commentary.

Of course, you want to make sure that you have high quality products and that all the other parts of the business go well. **But in the end it all comes down to sales.** So ask yourself how you can increase your overall sales results. What kind of measures can be taken to increase sales?

With more money in the bank, you have more options. You can develop new products and get into new markets. You can improve the quality of your products.

But without money, there is nothing you can do. Money or cash flow in a business is like the blood in a human body. It needs to flow and be plentiful. Otherwise, you will die of a heart attack.

> *Every one of your people is in sales and customer service,*
> *no matter what their job titles says.*

Nothing is worse that contacting a company and getting bad service. Your people cannot be rude or incompetent. Whoever is answering the phones must always be focused on customer service and satisfaction. Remember: everything counts. Especially, when there is a problem that needs to be fixed. The way a regular administrative person is handling a problem will determine the whole reputation of your company.

Keys to building a high-profit business

> *There is no secret of success. That is the secret.*

The main secret to business success is to follow the same steps (copy) that others have done. **Success is a series of small steps and goals that need to be achieved and done on a daily basis.** Everything that you want to achieve is doable. The secret of your success is determined by your daily agenda.

The greatest day in your life is when you take total responsibility for our attitudes. That's the day you truly grow up to become great.

> *All business skills are learnable.*
> *You can learn everything you need to know*
> *to build and run a successful business.*

In order to increase your profits, you need to get your numbers right.

How can you increase your profits and improve your ROI (return on investment)? Where do you need to cut cost, increase sales and boost profits? How can you beat your competition?

The answer is "The 1000% formula". The goal of the 1000% formula is to increase your productivity, performance and income more than ten times over ten years.

It is basically a steady and continuous improvement in each area that counts for business success. **You need to improve each area by 10% per year in order to increase your business by ten times.** 10% is a very realistic number and doable.

The key is to have a laser focus when it comes to your goals and numbers. Analyze every area in your business and make it your goal to improve each area by 10% as the initial goal.

> *If you improve several areas at once by 10%*
> *your overall success will be extraordinary.*

Building strategic relationships and alliances

> *All Business is People Business*

Form strategic alliances. Work with other people and organizations to be more successful. Look for people with successful track records.

Ask yourself where or with whom you could build strategic alliances. Which company could benefit from you and you from them? Is there a way to exchange customer lists? Is there a way to provide additional services from a different company that your customers also need?

The right kind of strategic partner can potentially make a huge difference. It can open up a whole new door of opportunities.

By traveling the world you also see other products and services. You can find people who can help you to produce your products much cheaper in a different country and help you to increase profits. **The world is full of opportunities and no matter where people are from they all want to succeed.** Building strategic alliances could be your number one advantage over the competition.

Leadership through change

Most people don't like change. They revolt against it unless they can clearly see the advantage it brings. For that reason, when good leaders prepare to take action or make changes, they take people through a process to get them ready for it.

The only constant in today's world is change. **As a leader you must always be prepared for change.** It has become a normal part of business life.

Ask yourself the following question: is there anything that I am doing in my business today that knowing what I now know, I wouldn't start up again today, if I had to do it over? If the answer is yes, then stop it immediately.

> *80% of all companies originally started with a different product.*

You must be open to accept the possibility that your products will have to change and that they will become obsolete one day.

Some companies have started with an entirely different kind of product or focus and eventually turned into a completely different company. They are extremely successful today with what they have but they originally started in a different industry.

Sometimes you must simply start to find out where the real market lies. But you would not have found out if you hadn't started in the first place.

Living your own dream

A scene from a typical soap opera looks like this:

09:05 pm: Vivian starts a new model agency

09:07 pm: Vivian rents an office the size of a tennis court

09:09 pm: Vivian hires a manager and goes to Hawaii for a holiday

Unfortunately, real business life is different. Vivian would have to talk to nine banks first and ask for a loan. On the weekends she would have to work part-time as a waitress and her first office would be the size of a small bathroom.

In order to live the dream of starting and running your own business enterprise you must start humble. **You will have to pay the price in advance for your dream.** You will face a lot of initial difficulties and obstacles but if you keep your head high and your attitude positive you will eventually get there.

When you start out, you will eventually hire a personal assistant. That is when things will take off and when you can focus on building your company. Making the strategic decision to hire people will change everything. Go confidently in the direction of your dreams and make it happen!

Falling forward – turning your mistakes into stepping-stones for success

Embrace past failures. Without failure there is no achievement.

People don't just fall into success. They need to have the intention to make things happen. It is not a matter of luck. It is not like having a lottery ticket. No one ever became a success by accident. Don't think: if I just hang around enough, something will happen.

Everyone has past failures. Don't condemn those failures. Those **failures were important to show you how it is not done. They helped you to learn what you needed to change.**

A success story is always much more interesting if you can say that you were broke, had a lot of problems and obstacles to overcome but in the end you made it happen because of your positive mental attitude, hard work and belief in your abilities.

Success: expectation vs. reality

> *Success is never a straight line going up. You can even use your past failures in your marketing message to give it more credibility.*

My own story is like that, too. I became a multi-millionaire in 2 ½ years and lost it all.

There was a time when I was so broke afterwards and emotionally depressed, it was unbelievable. But I got back on the horse and recovered from my past dark times.

I don't hide it. I mention it and embrace it. **The message that everyone can go through difficult times and recover, should give people hope and encouragement. It is not the end of the world.**

Many successful people made millions, lost them again and then made it again. Some of them went broke several times before they finally stayed on the top. It is not a shame and failure doesn't define you. It makes you stronger. **So embrace it and learn from it.**

Taking calculated risks as a leader

> *"The biggest risk is not taking any risk.*
> *In a world that is changing really quickly,*
> *the only strategy that is guaranteed to fail is not taking risks."*
> (Mark Zuckerberg)

People who take risks make about two big mistakes per year. People who avoid risks make about two big mistakes per year!

So you see, it doesn't help if you try to avoid risks at all cost.

The problem by always trying to avoid risk is that your negative thinking and attitude. Life is never secure. Things can always change and go differently than we anticipate.

> *You need to take risk to move forward. There is no other way.*

Business is all about being courageous.

But don't be stupid when taking risks. Use your head and common sense. When you send a sign to the Universe of your intention, things will work in your favor.

> *Show the world and the Universe*
> *that you are not scared of big numbers.*

Always think like a chess player

> *"Leaders establish the vision for the future*
> *and set the strategy for getting there."*
> (John P. Kotter)

Strategic planning is worthless unless there is first a strategic vision. **One of the main qualities of a good leader is analytical thinking.** You always need to think like a chess player and be very strategic in your approach.

In order to develop an entrepreneurial mindset **you need to constantly ask yourself what could go wrong and then have a plan for it.** This is not negative thinking at all. It is being prepared and feeling confident that you know in any situation or scenario what needs to be done. You have thought about all kinds of possible moves and outcomes in advance.

"If this happens, then I will do that. If that happens, then I will do this..." and so on. That should be your way of thinking. **Nothing should come as a surprise because you planned and prepared for all potential options and dangers.**

You should also plan and prepare for situations that could potentially damage your reputation. Sometimes you need to plan an exit strategy for yourself and put the blame on somebody else if things go south. That is not always very pleasant but sometimes it is necessary. Sometimes a chess player has to sacrifice a figure on purpose in order to win the game.

My friend and mentor, David Garcia, is especially strong in reality based strategic thinking. His ability to see things as they really are and not as you wish them to be and then make the right strategic decision is his biggest strength. Because of this ability alone, he became a multi-millionaire.

Always start with the end result in mind. What is going to be your exit strategy?

Unlock your Superconscious Mind

In order to generate ideas and achieve any goal, you must tap into the wisdom of the Universe. Remember that everything starts with a thought. **The more clear and positive your thoughts are, the more likely they will be manifested into the real life.**

In order to develop new ideas, eliminate mental blocks that hold you back and eliminate negative thinking, you need to take complete control of your thoughts and emotions.

You can't be constantly worried and act like a crazy person. You can't behave nervously and expect good things to happen. **You must take control of your emotions and your thoughts.**

You need to sit down calmly and write down on paper what exactly your current problems are or could be. Then you must write down possible solutions and contingency plans. You need to relax and see things clearly. You need to realize that there is a solution for every problem and you can't lose your inner peace.

Meditate or pray. Ask God or the Universe for help. **Do whatever helps you to stay calm and positive. Once you realize that, you can unlock your superconscious mind.** The Universe will help you to get ideas, solutions and bring the people, money and circumstances into your life to help you achieve your goals.

Personal qualities of a strategic leader

One of the best paradoxes of leadership is a leader's need to be both stubborn and open-minded. A leader must insist on sticking to the vision and stay on course to the destination. But he must be open-minded during the process.

Choosing a vision and deciding on a goal is the starting point for every leader. Some people are so stubborn that they lose their last shirt because of their own belief in their own dream. **In order to get to the top, you need to decide to get to the top but you also must be smart and change the course of action in case things don't work out as planned.** You don't need to change your goal but you must ask yourself why you have your goal in the first place. Why do you want to achieve it? Some people make a decision and then they are blind to everything else around them. Don't let that happen.

Sometimes you can go for a much better goal that will improve the quality of your life and have a lot less stress. Sometimes you must rethink your objectives and intentions. Some people put themselves under unnecessary stress.

Being successful means that you have found yourself and you are using your strengths. **You need to have a balance with work and your personal life.** Maybe all you need is to give yourself a little bit more time to achieve your goals to feel better about the process and not get so stressed out about it. If you don't give up and keep going in the right direction, you will eventually get there.

> *Join the 6 o'clock club.*
> *Get up every morning at 6 o'clock – no matter what.*

If you get up early, you can work out at the gym and get physically and emotionally fitter. You will need extra energy to become a great leader.

Get a coach or a mastermind group

One of the great secrets of successful people is that almost all of them have a role model or mentor that they look up to. If you know a person who is much more successful than you and it is someone that you respect, you should ask that person for advice. **Sometimes all you need is just one piece of information from a more successful person in order to make it to the top.**

Someone who has gone before you can teach you how it is done. **Successful people will always help other people who are serious about getting to the top.** They know how hard it is if you have to figure it out all by yourself. They know in what shoes you are in because one day they were in the same shoes.

> *Sometimes one idea, one insight or one piece of information can change everything.*

But if you get a piece of advice, you must follow it. Sometimes unsuccessful people will ask a successful person for advice and then they are told to read a certain book for example. More often than not, that person doesn't read the book and keeps coming back with questions.

Don't waste someone's time and think that they will do it for you. No one will do it for you. You must be grateful for advice and be open to accept it.

It also makes sense to meet once a month with a group of people who are on a similar level like you. Together you are much smarter and you can bounce off ideas to each other. **People who care about you will honestly tell you if your plans or ideas make sense or not.**

Leading your people

> *People may hear your words, but they feel your attitude.*

You must believe in your own vision and in yourself in order to get other people excited. **Your body language doesn't lie. It doesn't matter what you say. It matters how you say it.** If you are excited, people will feel it and then they will follow you – even if things are not perfect.

In order to motivate your people, you must encourage them. You must believe in them, too. It is a two-way street.

> *"A word of encouragement from a teacher to a child can change a life.*
> *A word of encouragement from a spouse can save a marriage.*
> *A word of encouragement from a leader*
> *can inspire a person to reach her potential."*
> (John C. Maxwell)

Some leaders ignore the fact that every person has hopes, dreams, desires, and goals of his own. And leaders must bring their vision and the aspirations of the people they lead together in a way that benefits everyone.

You can't go around and saying that you want to become a millionaire with the help of your people. That doesn't go well usually. You have every right to make money and become rich during the process but you must also improve the lives of your team.

You cannot be the only one who is benefiting from the company's success.

Your people should be part of it, too. Issue company stock options or make a bonus plan. Increase salaries and add benefits. Your business success should help many people to support their families, provide an education for their children and improve the lives of many others.

Difference between a boss and a leader

> *Leaders become great, not because of their power,*
> *but because of their ability to empower others.*

There is a big difference between a leader and a "boss". **A boss commands employees and depends on authority. A leader, however, develops people and generates enthusiasm. Leadership is influence.**

People will not follow you if you sit on your butt and command from behind the table. **Good leaders create a vision and then lead by example. They are always at the front lines and fight harder for the organization than anyone.**

> *Being a leader is like being a lady.*
> *If you have to go around telling people you are one, then you aren't.*

Don't talk too much. **Show your people how it is done.**

Things always cost twice as much and take twice as long as expected

When starting a new business or project everyone is always very optimistic and motivated. That is good because rarely do things go exactly as planned.

> *Most new projects cost twice as much*
> *and take twice as long as originally expected.*

When you make a new plan always know this rule, you can plan much better and with a lot less stress. **There are always unexpected costs or obstacles that make things take longer or costing more.**

That is normal and the sooner you can accept that, the faster you can move on.

At first, everyone is excited about a new project and we all have the tendency to set a high goal when we are in a happy and upbeat mood. Make sure that you can give yourself a safe and realistic time line for it achievement. It is better to communicate a time line that is further in the future and then to achieve the goal earlier.

The way you communicate a new goal or project with your team can make you or break you. So don't put yourself under too much pressure and expectations if it is not absolutely necessary.

Creating an automatic business system

> ## *The system is the solution. Not the people.*

In order to make a business successful you must realize that it is the system on how sales are being generated that matters most. McDonald's, for example, is a master enterprise in executing its system. Their hamburgers are not necessarily the best burgers in the world but because of the systems, McDonald's is the most successful hamburger chain in the world.

You need to have processes in place that ordinary people can execute. **People need to be exchangeable in a position. If a business is dependent on a particular person, then there is a big potential risk of loss.** Build an automatic business system where every position is clearly defined in an operations manual.

If you want to sell your business one day, but the business only works because of your person, then it is not a very good position to be in. **Create processes and remove yourself from the process. Just lead the company.**

When you start a new company, you must define from the beginning who is in which position. **Even if you are only two people at first, it must be clear who is the CEO and who has a different role.**

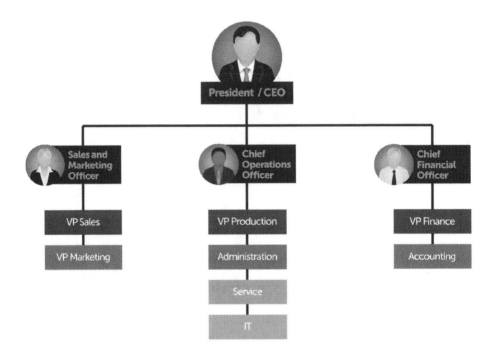

Even though there might be several positions and jobs, they must be filled with one name only. If your organization grows, you can give up some roles to new employees. The positions always stay the same but the faces change. Build a prototype for 5000 other branches.

Your goal should be to create a system that can be duplicated and started in a different city or region. In order to create a business system, you must use leverage. Leverage can be the manpower of other people, your sales channels, the money of other people, the knowledge of other people or the power of the Internet.

> *If you want to make more money and increase profits, you must expand the system. Open up more branches and hire more people who can generate more sales.*

The quality of your questions is key. A question like: "Why does this always happen to me?" is not helpful and your subconscious mind will always try to give you an answer like: "Because you are such a loser!"

Be more creative with your questions. Ask things like:

- How can I make $10,000 more by the end of the month?
- What process could be automated so that I don't constantly need to be involved?
- What else could I sell to make a profit?

You can achieve much more that you believe.

> *What you can normally do in one year, can be done in three months.*
> *What you can normally do in three months, can be done in two weeks.*

Everything you need to know is already inside of you. **Just ask the right questions and find the right answers. You will be amazed what can happen if you do just that.**

CHAPTER 3

BUILDING A **SUCCESSFUL TEAM**

Introduction

> **Leadership cannot really be taught. It can only be learned.**

Being a great leader really means to build the right team. Without the right people a company or organization is nothing. You cannot be a great leader on your own. Finding the right people and getting them to perform on a high level is a challenging task. People and personalities are so different and it is a difficult job to get them to work in harmony and work towards a common goal.

The goal of this brochure is to identify the steps necessary to build a successful team. Like in every sports team, for example, you will need stars, people who are the backbone and perform consistently and new people who need to be developed.

In the following steps you will learn some of the lessons that I have learned from building and running several sales teams and organizations.

Ways to recruit the best people

> **Hire people who are better than you are.**

The very core of every organization is your team. You need to try to hire and keep the best people. The better the quality of your people, the better is the team and in the end the result.

When your team has a large workload, it's important to have enough people "on board" to cope with it. But filling a vacant role too quickly can be a disastrous mistake.

Hurrying recruitment can lead to recruiting the wrong people for your team: people who are uncooperative, ineffective or unproductive. They might also require additional training, and slow down others on your team. With the wrong person, you'll have wasted valuable time and resources if things don't work out and they leave.

But what is worse is that other team members will be stressed and frustrated by having to "carry" the under-performer.

You need to hire people who will learn quickly because they are intelligent and who will not need constant handholding.

Your job has changed – you need to build a team now

Once you become a leader or manager, your responsibilities are very different from those you had before. A lot of new managers misunderstand their new role.

However, it's easy to forget that your job has changed, and that you now have to use a different set of skills to be effective. **This leads to you not doing what you've been hired to do – leading and managing.**

In your previous job you might have been a great sales person but now you need to focus on hiring new people and training them.

You need to learn how to effectively delegate and to lead by example.

> *Since your job has changed you will need a new set of skills.*

You should read books on leadership, go to seminars and ask other leaders for advice.

Personal sales results versus team sales result

One of the biggest mistakes that new leaders make is to stop making sales themselves and focusing solely on their team.

> *Typically, the best sales person advances to become team leader. Then the mistake is that he stops making sales on his own because he believes that he now must only focus on his new people.*

But the problem is that the result and the amount of money that he earns is going down too much because he doesn't understand when to focus on the team and when to still make sales on his own.

The following chart should illustrate how much personal sales a new team leader should do and how much of the income should come from the team.

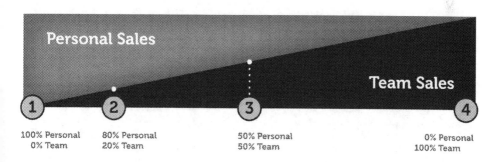

1) In the beginning when there are no people, 100% of the result must come from personal sales.
2) Once he has a few people to lead, still 80% must come from his own personal efforts and only 20% comes from the team.
3) In the third phase when he has more people it is about 50% and 50%.
4) Once the team grows higher in numbers, he can stop making personal sales and then solely focus on the team.

> **The most common mistake is that new team leaders stop making personal sales once they get the title team leader.**

I personally would say that if the number of sales people is anywhere from 10 to 15 people is the moment when you can stop making personal sales and only focus on the team and not earlier. I used to lead over 25 people directly as a team leader and managed them well. That is when I stopped with my personal sales and only helped the team.

Delegating and Supervising

Some managers don't delegate, because they feel that no one apart from themselves can do key jobs properly. This can cause huge problems as work bottlenecks around them and as they become stressed and burned out.

Delegation does take a lot of effort up-front, and it can be hard to trust your team to do the work correctly. But unless you delegate tasks, you are never going to have time to focus on the overall picture that most leaders and managers are responsible for.

Also, you will fail to develop your people so that they can take the pressure off you. In order to do a successful delegation you need to make sure that you check a couple of days after if the job has been done properly or not.

Write down everything and make sure to double check afterwards.

Also, you should encourage people to come back with questions if they are unsure of how to complete the task but don't take on the task. Otherwise they will never learn it and you will be stressed out because you are doing everybody's job.

The four phases of leadership

First phase: *Directing*

The leader provides specific direction and closely monitors task accomplishment. Involves clearly telling people what to do, how to do it, when to do it, and then closely monitoring their performance: for people who lack competence but are enthusiastic and committed.

Second phase: *Coaching*

The leader continues to direct and closely monitor accomplishments, but also explains decisions, solicits suggestions, and supports progress: for people who have some competence but lack commitment.

Third phase: *Supporting*

The leader facilitates and supports people's efforts toward task accomplishment and shares responsibility for decision-making with them: Involves listening to people, providing support and encouragement for their efforts, and then facilitating their involvement in problem-solving and decision-making: for people who have competence but lack confidence or motivation.

Fourth phase: *Delegating*

The leader turns over responsibility for decision-making and problem solving to people: for people who have both competence and commitment.

Turning average people into great people

> *Unfortunately, you never know whether you have a great person or an average to below-average performing person when you hire someone new.*

I have had new people and thought that they were the new superstars and it turned out that they were all talk and created no results. And then I also had people of whom I wasn't sure and they turned out to be great. Unfortunately, they don't have it written on their forehead when you first hire them. **You need to hire them and then you will find out.**

I have trained many average people well and they turned into good and solid producers. The keys to turning average people into great people are the following things:

1. **High expectations and work load in the beginning**
2. **High producing peers and fast-paced environment**
3. **Communicating expectations of what needs to be done**
4. **Extensive training plan**
5. **Daily contact and immediate corrections of behavior**

It is important that the first three months are very hard for the new employee. You need to overload him with work and expectations. But you also must give him everything that he needs to succeed. An extensive training plan is important and training and enabling is more important in the beginning than motivation.

The last step is to let him "fall into the cold water". This means that he will either learn to swim or drown. But you can only do this after the first three months. That is where you will see who has what it takes. You are not allowed to "baby" the person anymore after the initial period. The communication and frequency of contact will change because you have to focus on developing new people then.

Expectation versus self-responsibility

When people start in a new organization they have all kinds of expectations. One of the main things is that they feel that it is your job and responsibility to teach them everything. If they don't perform, then they blame you for not giving them the right tools.

But this kind of behavior is not the behavior of winners. You need to teach your people that even though you are trying to teach them the basics and give them the tools necessary to perform, you will forget things from time to time.

They need to be made aware that it is not your responsibility that they have everything but theirs. If they are missing a tool or missing something that is hindering them to perform well, then they must come to you with their request.

A lot of new people wait for the team leader to come to them and then they blame the team leader for their failure.

> *So teach your people self-responsibility. If they want something, they must come to you and not the other way around.*

Motivating people to peak performance

> *The task of the leader is to get his people from where they are to where they have not been.*

As a manager and leader you must ask yourself where your employee is doing a good job and in which areas he is weak.

If an employee is not reaching his sales targets than it is always one of two reasons:

1. He is simply not good enough in the basic sales elements like prospecting, presenting, closing, etc. (not technical or product knowledge)

2. His mental attitude is wrong. I have found that most people want to be successful but they are not able because of lack of training in the basic sales elements.

Make sure that you check the basic sales elements like prospecting on the phone, setting enough first meetings, presentation skills, time frame of a meeting (too long or too short), closing techniques and other factors. **Really analyze and ask about details in each area until you find out where the problem for his lack of sales is.**

> ### You will only be able to make positive changes
> ### if you really know what the problem is.

Sometimes we like a person so much and we believe so much in his future potential that we forget that he is still a rookie and learning the basic sales elements.

You need to make sure to teach each one of your people so well that they become great communicators and that they do the things that work.

> ### Selling is a skill-based profession that can be learned by anyone.
> ### If the employee is good at selling but still not making progress
> ### then check his attitude.

Realistic view of the situation

> ### "Face reality as it is, not as it was or as you wish it to be."
> (Jack Welch)

This is one of the most important lessons in business life. A lot of new managers do wishful thinking and then wonder why things don't change. Only if you take a very hard and realistic view on things you can identify what is wrong or what could go wrong with a situation.

Being realistic doesn't mean being negative. It is actually the opposite. By identifying the REAL STEPS to what needs to be done you can make REAL POSITIVE CHANGES. Anything else is wishful thinking and fantasy.

You also need to do realistic goal setting for your people. They will always give you their sales target but in reality it is always about 60% of what they tell you. So your team budget is the sum of all budgets and then 60% of that. Now your job is to find out what you could do to improve that number.

> *A team takes on the personality of the head coach.*

Once you have trained your people to face problems with a realistic view, they will be able to make real improvements. All the positive thinking and attitude is important when it comes to goal setting but when it comes to analyzing a problem situation, you need to put on the glasses that give you the real view.

Increase the average sales result per person

> *A good objective of leadership is to help those who are doing poorly to do well and to help those who are doing well to do even better.*

Your goal as the manager is to improve each sales person's results by 10% per month. You can't expect people to change from one month to the next. Sometimes it will take some time until they are getting better. But you need to improve an area that is weak so that they will make progress. If you help each person a little bit each month, the overall team result will dramatically improve. **Try to identify what is holding someone back.** Usually, the one thing where they do poorly is their weakest link and that is the reason why the overall result is not satisfactory.

Many clients versus elephant hunting

> *The top salesperson in the organization probably missed*
> *more sales than 90% of the sales people on the team,*
> *but they also made more calls than the others made.*

Elephant hunting means going only after the biggest clients. The idea sounds good but in reality it always turns into a disaster situation. This happens to all sales people. They have one huge client and they spend all their time and energy on this client. They believe that this will be their big breakthrough and once the client is secured, everything will be great.

But in the meantime they fail to contact other clients because they rely on this big client. And the result is in 99% of the cases the same: The client doesn't come and the person's sales result for the month is **ZERO.**

I have seen it happening all the time and it happened to me, too. **Elephant hunting doesn't work.**

In order to get big clients, you need to contact many clients and by the law of averages you will eventually have a big client in your portfolio. Getting big clients is a normal part of business but they are random and seldom. **Out of 50 clients you will have one big one. But if you don't take the other 49 clients, you will fail miserably.**

Quantity = Quality

In order to get quality leads you need to contact a lot of people. In order to get great sales people for your team, you need to hire a lot of people. You cannot go after quality alone in order to get quality.

That is a myth. You will get quality by going for quantity. Think about it. It is a mathematical law. The more people you contact, the higher the chances that better people are among it. The less people you contact, the less chances you will have to get good people.

> *Luck doesn't exist. Luck is the result of hard work and contacting many people. You will get lucky if you contact MANY people.*

A, B and C

We used to categorize our clients into A-clients, B-clients and C-clients:

- **A-clients** have the highest income and they are the best clients and they will give you the highest amount of sales and commissions.

- **B-clients** are good and solid and you can work well with them but they are not rich.

- **C-clients** are bad clients. They have little money and you can't make a high commission with them.

The more A and B-clients you have, the better. People who mostly have C-clients have poor sales results. **Now here is the interesting part:**

> *It takes exactly the same amount of time and effort to deal with an A-client as it takes with a C-client.*

So why not focus only on A-clients? (Not elephant hunting but great clients nonetheless). And here is the second epiphany for you:

A-clients know other A-clients that you can get referred to. B-clients know B and C-clients BUT c-clients only know other C-clients or even D-clients.

Once you are in the wrong circle it is hard to get out of it. So focus your efforts on the right group. But this also means that you must be absolutely professional so that you can handle the big clients.

Each employee needs to be treated differently

> *"Management is about arranging and telling.*
> *Leadership is about nurturing and enhancing."*
> (Tom Peters)

The title "boss" is not always really a good thing. It also means, "to serve your people" and "being responsible if things go wrong". **You cannot be like a military leader and give orders.**

That usually doesn't work well in a sales organization. People are driven by emotions and the fear of rejection and failure will often paralyze people. That is why you must be able to lead each employee differently. You must know what they need or where they have a hard time.

You need to develop a sixth sense and strong emotional channel to see what is wrong and where they need help. Rules need to be in place but rules don't always have to be enforced blindly.

Leadership for results

> *"Effective leadership is not about making speeches or being liked;*
> *leadership is defined by results not attributes."*
> (Peter Drucker)

In the end all that counts are results. If you want to lead your team to success you must make sure that your people are productive. It doesn't matter how great you are in giving speeches or how popular you are among your people.

If they are not producing results, then all the show doesn't help. It is better to be hands-on with your employees and actually help them to close a deal than to give another motivational speech.

Strategic management

There is one simple rule when it comes to business success:

> *A company is successful if it has a lot of sales and it has problems when it has a lack of sales.*

Everything else in between is secondary. It doesn't matter how good the company's product and services are or how beautiful your marketing material is, in the end all the counts are sales and profits. In order to have a successful organization, you must focus on developing strategies that lead to sales success. If your company is suffering, then the main reason that it comes down to is always a lack of sales. You need to focus on generating new clients and then every other problem within the organization can be solved. It is as simple as that.

Praise and recognition

> *"You don't lead by hitting people over the head -that's assault, not leadership."*
> (Dwight D. Eisenhower)

The secret to success is good leadership, and good leadership is all about making the lives of your team members or workers better. People need praise and recognition to feel appreciated and to be motivated. A good leader understands that the psychological state of his people is responsible for the overall result. By giving your people a lot of praise and recognition, you will get better results. If you constantly criticize and condemn people they will eventually perform worse.

The critical differences

> *"No institution can possibly survive if it needs geniuses or supermen to manage it. It must be organized in such a way as to be able to get along under a leadership composed of average human beings."*
> (Peter Drucker)

In order to succeed in selling a product, a company must have clear procedures in place so that the product can be sold successfully. **The system itself must be well organized and it must be possible for average people with and average intelligence to make money.**

If it is very difficult to make a sale and only people who are specialists can do it, then it will be hard to duplicate and multiply a sales process. Therefore you must change your approach.

> *"It is true that integrity alone won't make you a leader, but without integrity you will never be one."*
> (Zig Ziglar)

Honesty and integrity are the single most important factors for a leader. If he is caught lying about something, he will lose all respect and credibility. Without an honest leadership you cannot get very far.

You don't need to communicate every single bad event that is happening and that people don't need to know but you cannot lie about it or cover it up if it is an integral part of their daily work. Sooner or later people will find out and then it will be a lot worse and telling the truth about a problem or situation.

So as a leader you must keep your integrity at all times. Without it, you are nothing.

How to fire an employee

Firing an employee is never a fun experience. But unfortunately it has to be done once in a while.

> ### The rule is hire slow and fire fast.

The main reason why you need to fire an employee fast is because of the potential that he will negatively influence other employees. **Don't ever keep a person with a bad attitude who is creating a negative environment** just because he still needs to fulfill his contract. The damage that he will do is much greater by sticking around.

Just pay him for his remaining days and let him go immediately. Don't wait.

Also, if someone is a good person but they are not making any sales, then they don't make any money. It is your social responsibility to fire this person in order to avoid destroying his financial life completely. **Just because this person is loyal to you doesn't mean that he is in the right position.**

Don't make the mistake of firing too many people at once. This will weaken your organization more than you think. It will create a negative energy and losing too many people will hurt your sales result.

> *The correct way to fire someone is always to do in a positive manner.*
> *You say things like: "I personally really like you but I think you would be*
> *happier somewhere else."*

Also, if you want to get rid of someone who is underperforming, you need to make a written goal plan for the next week of the things that need to be done. Both parties need to sign that piece of paper and he needs to make a promise to achieve these goals.

Since there is an attitude problem anyway, you already know that he is not going to achieve his goals next week. But because you have it in writing and he agreed to do it, you can hold him accountable for it later. **This will be the reason why he will get fired. He was unable to achieve his targets.**

Get rid of negative people who emotionally block you or drain your energy

In every organization there are people who are very smart or even great producers but they are difficult to deal with. Either they are constantly negative or they undermine your authority in some way.

Since it is your job and you also must be happy with the people that work for you, **you need to rid yourself from negative people.** Sometimes people don't particularly do anything wrong but they emotionally block you and your positive energy. If that is the case then you must get rid of them – no matter what the cost. Even if it hurts financially, it will hinder you to work well with the other employees.

If you catch someone talking negatively to others, you must also get rid of that person. There are people who are always negative and they influence new or other employees negatively. You cannot allow any negative talking people who hurt the organization. Fire them on the spot.

Sometimes you need to fire someone and you must do it in front of everyone to set an example for the remaining employees. **Only do this once.** But then you will get the reputation that they can't dance on your nose and your overall discipline will be much higher.

2 types of managers – pioneers and process-oriented managers

> *"People who don't take risks generally make about two big mistakes a year. People who do take risks generally make about two big mistakes a year."*
> (Peter Drucker)

There are two types of managers in every organization. **There are people who are really good at starting up a new organization.** They are the pioneer type who can build up a brand new team and start an organization with a lot of power and dynamic energy.

And then there is the type of manager who is really good at managing and organizing people once they are there. This type is much more process oriented and can manage the every day operations better than the pioneer would do. Ask yourself which type of manager you really are.

If you are better at the pioneer stage then you should focus your strengths on that. If you prefer to manage an existing organization then your choices are different. Which type are you?

Set visionary goals

> *You cannot expect to fly with the eagles if you are on the ground looking for corn with the chickens.*

The final step to becoming a great leader who can build a great organization is to excel with your team. You need to aim high and live for a grand vision. You need to motivate yourself and your team with a greater vision and purpose and you must want to get to the top.

Not everyone is going to be able to follow you but if you have the right kind of dreamers in your team, you will have people who will excel and go very far with you. If you can find your **top five people** who can manage others teams, you will be able to build an organization that is very big.

Here is what I mean:

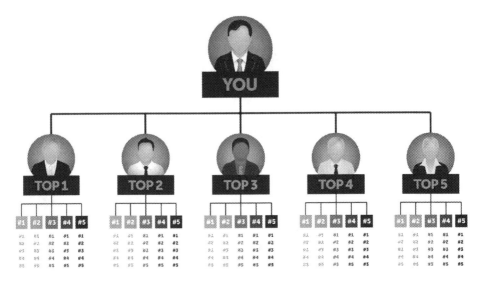

If you are able to find the **5 key people** who will be your main managers, help them to find their **top 5 key people** and then you will have built an organization of more than 150 people who can lead others and continue to build teams underneath you. **You cannot achieve success alone.** You will need a strong leadership team that will help you.

The higher quality your Top 5 is, the stronger your organization. This principle alone has built sales organizations with thousands of people.

CHAPTER 4

MOTIVATION
FOR YOUR
EMPLOYEES

Introduction

> *"People often say that motivation doesn't last.*
> *Well, neither does bathing - that's why it is recommend daily.*
> (Zig Ziglar)

Motivation of your employees is a key ingredient when it comes to building a successful organization. In order to achieve greater results, **you must know and understand how to motivate your people.** The same things don't motivate everyone and it is important to apply a variety of tools and techniques to get your employees to perform better. It is your job as a leader to motivate the whole team and to find out what motivates and drives each employee individually. If you can create a motivating work environment for your employees, they will be happier and perform better, which is good for you. If you fail to motivate your people, it will eventually create a negative environment and the end of the organization won't be too far.

I have put together a variety to ideas and tools that I have used in the past. I have also learned and understood what drives people and how important and essential the right kind of motivation can be.

External motivation versus internal motivation

> *You can look for external sources of motivation and that can catalyze*
> *a change, but it won't sustain one. It has to be from an internal desire.*

You can motivate people all day long but once you stop motivating them, they will stop producing results. **In the beginning, the motivation is external and must come from the leader.** But it needs to be your goal to find out what really drives them.

Eventually, they need to be able to have an internal motivation.

If someone doesn't have internal motivation, you cannot help him or her in the long run. Your employees must develop it or find it themselves. **People who are unable to motivate themselves must be content with mediocrity, no matter how impressive their other talents are.**

Don't just motivate your people – enable them by teaching them

> *Try to hire people you don't have to motivate.*
> *But once you hired them, you should motivate them anyway.*

The biggest motivation for people is to create actual results. The best way to create results is to enable people by teaching and training them on how to do it. This is especially true for sales people. If you help someone to become better in their sales script so that he is able to make more sales, you will achieve a much higher level of motivation than if you tried to simply motivate him with words alone.

Success is a series of smaller steps or mini-goals that need to be achieved. If you help your employee to reach a number of smaller goals each day, he is able to move forward and that will motivate him because it gives him momentum. I am all for motivation and encouraging words but you need to help your employee to reach goals by training him properly. You need to teach him and give the tools to be able to do the job.

The better is he trained, the more likely he is going to produce results.

People quit eventually because they lack results. All the talk and motivation is not helping them to achieve results. In real estate they say that the number one rule is: location, location, location. But in sales and business it is: training, training, training!

Develop a vision for them and with them

> *If you are motivated enough and put the work in,*
> *you can achieve anything in life that you set your mind to.*

In order to motivate new people you must develop a long-term plan with them. You should create a vision for them where you plan for them to make money, climb the career ladder within the organization, get trained and find their place in the company. **You must help your people to see how they can be a part of your organization for the next few years and how it will benefit them in their personal lives.**

If people have a long-term outlook it will affect how well they work and how motivated they are. They will take things more seriously and make more of an effort with clients and people in the organization. Some people want to climb the internal career ladder so badly that it will be their main driving force. **If you show them a way, they will work harder and perform better in their current position.**

Incentives

Incentives like a paid trip by the company to the Bahamas or Europe for a week are also great motivational tools. When I was still in Europe, we had a yearly trip to Palm Beach, Florida where we would spend a week in a super luxurious villa. This trip was so exciting and on the highest level of quality that it motivated almost everyone.

The goal of a trip like this is that people need to qualify for it over several months. In order to go on that trip and to qualify for it, you must have a consistent sales result on a high level. Since it won't be possible for everyone to achieve this goal, it makes it special and the ones that want to go on that trip will focus their efforts on the necessary requirements. Some people will achieve exceptional results in the last month during the qualification period in order to make the trip.

If you make a destination a regular thing and some people come back to tell others how great the trip was, it will motivate the newer employees to join the next year.

Money

> *Money is only a tool. It is not the money itself that will motivate people. It is the freedom that money will give them that drives them.*

Money is a huge factor for everyone. Let us not kid ourselves here. Most people have a certain job because of money and not necessarily because they love what they are doing.

Since we live in a society where you need money for everything and money can make your life better, you should create an organization where people have the opportunity to make more money by performing better.

You should always have a performance-oriented kind of working environment where you can make more money by helping to make more profits for the organization. Some companies work with yearly bonuses and that can be extremely powerful to keep employees and to motivate them. Create clear rules on how to earn a yearly bonus and then be generous at the end of the year.

When it comes to Christmas money, be very generous. **There is nothing worse than being cheap** – especially during this time of year where everyone is more pensive and thinking about their life and the upcoming new year.

In order to get a closer connection with some people you can always create a ritual where you give them their salary or check in person during a private talk. They will start to link money (= happy emotion) with you and that you are the provider. This way you will have a more powerful psychological impact and association as a leader.

Lists and rankings

> *In order to motivate sales people in an organization,*
> *you must have a daily, weekly and monthly list*
> *with the sales results on the wall for everyone to see.*

This is one of the most powerful tools. **Some people live for the list on the wall.** Since everybody can see what the sales result is, there are some people who strive to be number one.

This type of motivation is so strong that they will work hard and do almost anything to be on the top of the list.

The recognition among their peers and in the organization is extremely important for some people. People who don't perform well are embarrassed to be at the bottom of the list and it will drive them to move up.

Lists and rankings are not to be underestimated. It shows some of the weak sales people that it is possible to generate a higher income result and it will give you the tools that you need to motivate them.

Some of the negative people who try to tell you that it is not possible to make more sales will lose their argument because **it will be public knowledge how well some other people perform each month.**

Praise and recognition

> *"People will die for ribbons."*
> (Napoleon)

You should create an environment where people get recognition for their results. **You should honor people each month or each week in a group meeting in front of everyone.** You can honor them by mentioning them in your speech or by getting them to the front and ask them questions about their achievement.

You should use the opportunity to give praise to your people as much as possible. You should also encourage your employees to give praise to their peers. **If you create a positive environment where people get a lot of praise instead of jealousy and competition, you will have a much better organization.**

Competition can also be positive and healthy. If you communicate it well and get two people or groups to compete against each other for the "winner of the week" award for example, you can motivate them to perform exceptionally well. Once the week is over, you should have a little team ceremony where you hand out a trophy or diploma or give them a check. But make sure to give praise out in front of everyone.

Career steps and levels

You should create a system where there are many little career steps and levels and you can give them a promotion and hand out a diploma. This is something that is used very well in many sales organizations.

The person is still a sales person but he moves up from rookie, to sales person level 1 to level 2 and so on. By climbing the ladder he will get a higher percentage on his commission.

People take pride within the organization to be on a higher level than others. You can give them pins or work with colors so that they can be recognized.

You should also have an "active status" so that people will remain on their career level and don't drop down with their performance. This is a minimum sales result in order to maintain the commission level.

> *Some people want to become team leader so badly because they want to become a "boss". The motivation to become team leader can be a huge driving force for some employees.*

Again, these tools motivate not everyone but surprisingly a lot of people are. **You never know which tool works on which employee. But using many different motivational tools you can cover almost everybody.**

Everything is a numbers game

> *"Start with good people, lay out the rules, communicate with your employees, motivate them and reward them. If you do all those things effectively, you can't miss."*
> (Lee Iacocca)

As a leader you should know that when it comes to sales, it is all a numbers game. **The more calls are being made, the better the sales result.**

The more people that you can motivate to do sales-oriented activities; the better the end result will be. The more people you have in your organization, the higher the end result will be.

> *In the end it all comes down to people and the amount of clients that they can contact.*

Your job is to motivate your people to contact as many clients as possible.

Personal talk / meeting

If you are sitting down with an employee to have a personal meeting, you should structure your meeting like this:

1. Green round: 5 to 10 minutes
2. Questions and analysis
3. New information or teach new skill
4. Motivation, delegation and control

We call it the **green round** because of the personality type color green that states that your should focus on rapport and friendly talk. Don't shoot straight into the conversation. Talk about his private life, his hobbies and interests or his family. Make sure you can feel him out and know in what kind of mood he is in at the moment.

In the second part you should **analyze his last month and his activities**. You should ask a lot of questions to find out what he did well and where he needs improvement.

In the next part you could either **communicate important new information about the company or teach him a new skill that will help him to get better.**

In the last part you need to **motivate him and get him to commit to a higher sales target** than last month.

Team meetings

> ### The goal of a team meeting is to motivate your people.

I remember when our team meetings started out with a guy showing us pictures of red Ferraris, expensive mansions and jewelry. Since we were a dynamic group of sales people who were mainly motivated by money and things, it worked for about 80% of us to get us excited.

Even though everybody knew that we were being motivated on purpose, we didn't care and loved seeing those pictures and dreaming about the future.

But **in a team meeting you must use all kinds of tools to motivate your people.** You can motivate some of them with money and things, others with facts and new developments in the company, others with incentives, others with a new product, others with getting more involved in new projects and some with special praise and recognition.

Use the opportunity to honor certain people for their results of the previous month or week. Get them to stand up and come to the front and let them tell the group why they were so successful. Praise them and honor them in front of everybody. It will not only reinforce this person but also motivate and encourage others to want to perform well in the upcoming month to stand in front of the team and being given recognition.

Motivation with facts

> *"A strategy is something like, an innovative new product; globalization, taking your products around the world; be the low-cost producer. A strategy is something you can touch; you can motivate people with; be number one and number two in every business. You can energize people around the message."*
>
> (Jack Welch)

Your people need to have a high level of identification with the company. People who work for Apple for example, absolutely LOVE apple. They think that their products are absolutely the best and much better than Microsoft.

You need to figure out what your company stands for and that message or a specific service, product or trait can motivate people to work there.

Messages that motivate people are for example:

- Tradition
- Highest quality
- Special service
- Number one in your field or industry

People want to be proud to be working for a specific organization. They get more recognition and respect from their families and friends if they are associated with a certain company.

Work/life balance and other benefits of freedom

> *People want money and time – not just money.*

It seems that money is the only motivation in certain sales organizations. But money is only a key motivator for a certain amount of people. **Other things motivate a lot of people, too:**

1. Freedom to work from home
2. Flexible time schedule
3. Good benefits like health insurance or retirements plans
4. Free coffee, drinks and snacks in the office kitchen
5. Nice working environment *(beautiful office space, garden near office, ocean views, etc.)*
6. Status symbol *(address, location, professional looking environment and attire)*
7. More holidays or time off
8. Enabling parents to work and take care of their children *(company daycare, flexible hours)*
9. Company trips and vacation *(incentives)*
10. Overall mood and energy *(positive and happy environment)*

In order to motivate your people to stay in your organization, **you need to ask yourself what you would ideally have if you were working there and then create the circumstances.**

> *Only happy people are productive people.*

The money you invest into creating better conditions is well spent. You will gain more loyalty if you are generous with some basic things. Don't try to save on the vending machine or on drinks. This relatively small expense for the company can kill the overall motivation and mood if you make people pay for it.

Personal goal setting plan

> *"Goals are not only absolutely necessary to motivate us.*
> *They are essential to really keep us alive."*
> (Robert H. Schuller)

It should be a standard in your organization to develop a personal goal setting; career and income plan with each employee in the very beginning when someone joins the company.

Most people never really find out what they want and if you help them or even force them to develop personal goals, it will create a new energy that will drive them to achieve them.

Working in your company should be a tool to reach those goals. The harder they work and the more sales they make, the faster they can reach their goals.

You should even break down tasks like for example making specific number of phone calls and link them to reaching a specific goal. You could say that if you make 50 calls per day for the next six months, you will be able to buy your BMW M5 – no matter what the outcome of the calls is. This calculation is based on the numbers game of averages.

If someone is motivated by climbing the career ladder, you need to know that and you can use that each time you talk to them. Don't assume anything. Ask and write it down!

Each employee needs to be treated differently

In general, we all want the same things:

1. Love

2. Money

3. Beauty

4. Freedom

5. Recognition

6. Attention

> *As a leader, it is your job to find out
> what motivates each employee individually.*

The same things don't motivate everyone. That is why you must talk to each employee about his private situation and goals that he wants to achieve.

Some leaders make the mistake that all people need to be treated the same way and by the same rules. That is absolutely not true. **You have different personalities and with some people you must be more flexible than with others. You cannot apply the same rules to everyone and in the same manner.** Some people have ADD (attention deficit disorder) and it is almost not their fault that they cannot remember all the rules.

You need to find the right angle and motivation for each employee. You need to find out what drives them and how you can help them to reach their goals. You need to be more analytical and strategic with some employees while as with others you must motivate them with a red Ferrari picture.

Depending on the personality type of your employee, you must motivate each one differently.

Involvement with special projects

In motivating people, you've got to engage their minds and their hearts.

You can motivate people by leading by example and by being excited but also by having productive ideas to make them feel involved. Some people have great talents in certain areas and if someone can apply his special talents, he will feel honored and much more motivated to be in the organization.

Try to find out what special talents people have and see if it is possible to use them in the right way. People, who perform well, will be happier than people who perform poorly.

Company event once a month

It is important to get out of the office and go outside with the team once in a while. I would recommend doing a monthly night out where you either go out for dinner, go bowling or do some other fun activity.

Doing something outside of the office will increase the team building effect and people will have fun. This is much more important than most people believe.

An event in a different environment will give the people additional motivation and they associate your company with fun.

An event like bowling will increase the team spirit and people will appreciate it. After a bowling night most people will also go out to a bar or club, which might be additional fun. **Encourage them to go out together and build friendships. It will benefit the organization.**

But make sure that you behave yourself as the leader. Don't do crazy things or drink too much. People are still watching you and judging you. You cannot risk losing their respect. You can do something funny once in a while as an exception but don't go overboard.

Fun, laughter and a good time are very important factors for people to feel happy and content in your organization. The money that you spend on paying for these events are well worth it.

Leverage your motivation throughout the team and organization

> *"Motivation is everything. You can do the work of two people, but you can't be two people. Instead, you have to inspire the next guy down the line and get him to inspire his people."*
> (Lee Iacocca)

You can do something for someone and he will tell others what you have done. This will spread like a wild fire and if it is positive, it will have a positive effect in your organization.

If you have team leaders you must motivate your team leaders so that they can motivate their people. You need to use their leverage by communicating to them first.

Your suit, your car and your house can motivate others

> *"You've got to be before you can do and do before you can have."*
> (Zig Ziglar)

If people want to have the things that you already have, they will listen to you and try to do the same things that you have done to get them. If you drive a crappy car, you cannot expect that this car will motivate people. **No matter how much money you have in your bank account, a low-key lifestyle of understatement will not get people to follow you.** I don't necessarily mean that you need to go into debt to buy an expensive car to impress others but you need to be aware that people watch you all the time. **You cannot motivate them if they think you are not successful yourself.** They will not follow you or be motivated by your words. It is ok to drive a regular good car but make sure you don't drive a rusty piece of sh*t!

Sometimes a great car can be an investment into motivating your team and in making yourself feel like a million bucks. **As the leader you should be dressed perfectly. Little details like special cufflinks, a nice looking tie or a special watch can motivate your people.** It will not motivate all people but some who are driven by money and things.

It is also important in regards to your image where you live. If you preach about money and you live in the basement of your mother's old house in a bad neighborhood, you will not get any attention. In that case you should not let anybody know where you live at all.

So be aware how you dress, what you drive and what you do. Everything counts and everyone is watching and judging you all the time. Make sure that your things and your behaviors have no negative motivational effect your people.

Negative motivation versus positive motivation

> *"I always joke about letting the haters motivate you.*
> *Everybody has that in their life, people who doubt them or make them feel less than they are. It just takes faith and belief in yourself, and you've got to dig deep into that.*
> *That has to come from you - nobody's going to give you that."*
> (Jennifer Lopez)

In general, negative motivation is always stronger than positive motivation. If you want to lose weight, the reason is typically to avoid the negative comments or lack of love and attention that you are getting. It is not necessarily always because they want to look and feel better.

Some people were told that they were not good enough or that they would never reach a certain goal. Just to prove them wrong, people seem to be motivated. This motivation is so strong that they put everything into it.

Some people respond very well to this type of motivation. You will usually hear it out of the context when you talk to them more intimately. So you can use that to motivate them. You can say things like: "Never again!" and the employee will agree and that will be his motto.

Keep learning and improving yourself as a leader

> *If people can see that you are moving forward*
> *as well in your own development and career,*
> *they will also be motivated to follow your career path.*

Leaders must be close enough to relate to others, but far enough ahead to motivate them.

As a leader you must always know more than your people. You need to constantly be learning new skills and knowledge so that you will stay ahead of them. You need to work on your own personal development by becoming an active reader, by listening to audio programs or by going to seminars.

It is always best to be a leader who has walked the walk like his people before and knows what they are going through on a daily basis. If you know what it takes to make phone calls and to get rejection like your people, you will be much better able to relate to them.

If people can follow in your footsteps and can take your career as an example for themselves, they will try to get your job once you are moving up the ladder yourself. Your own success story will motivate your people to copy you.

Laziness means having no real goals

There are no lazy people. There are only people with no real goals.

Laziness is a myth. If someone is lazy is simply means that he is not motivated to do something. And the real reason is because he has no goals that motivate him enough.

Some people are not driven by all the tools like money, things or recognition like everybody else. It is your job to find out what really drives them.

Most people have never really thought about their goals and what they really want. They have a basic idea but they don't have clear written goals. **Your job is to create an intensive workshop with your people and really develop a list of goals that truly motivates them.**

Without goals people will not see the need to do more.

If they are comfortable where they are right now and there is no burning desire, then you won't have a chance to get them to perform better. Also make sure that they don't just take on your goals or the goals that you "should have".

The main reason why people don't do well is simply because they don't know what they want. Help them and it will change their lives!

CHAPTER 5

BECOMING A GREAT **SALES MANAGER** *AND LEADER*

My personal leadership experience with sales people

In my entire career I managed many employees and sales people. I started out in the biggest independent financial planning sales organization in Europe and worked my way up the ladder. In 1997 I was the number one team leader with the best sales result of my team. I competed against 1000 other team leaders in Europe and created a new sales record. I was promoted to sales manager and became one the top leaders in that organization. **I trained and managed around 75 sales people during that time and I was only 23 years old back then.**

When I went into the hedge fund industry I became the global sales manager for the biggest independent hedge fund company in the world. I managed a team of very bright and sometimes-arrogant young people with impressive University degrees and we **improved the overall sales team result from $42 million in a four month period to over $245 million just one year later.** Then later on I built my own sales teams and organization when I went into the Private Equity field and I managed over 60 people.

During my entire career I hired, fired, motivated, encouraged, trained, led, promoted, evaluated and educated a lot of new sales people and employees.

This program is a summary of my personal leadership experience. This knowledge is real and comes from actual experience from the business world.

So let's begin.

Keeping the numbers up

> *People tend to get better if you expect better things of them and if you treat them as if they were better already*
>
> (Karl Jaspers)

There is a big difference in your leadership style in how you lead your regular full-time employees or your sales people.

A regular full-time employee typically has a fixed salary and a very clear job description of what is expected of him or her.

A sales person who is working on commission requires a different kind of management style. There are rules that apply to both groups but this program will focus mainly on the leadership style of sales people or employees who are paid based on their performance.

A sales person who is working on commission needs to set appointments, meet with clients and close deals. Depending on the organization and its rules a sales person can make his own schedule. Therefore, if he is more motivated, he will make more appointments with clients and if he is frustrated he will make less appointments.

Also, if there are only sales targets and no targets in regards to the number of meetings with clients, it doesn't matter exactly how many meetings he is having if the sales target is reached. If he is not forced to make more meetings with clients, then he won't necessarily do them.

> *This is why the psychological and mental state of a sales person is the number one factor that determines whether he is successful or not.*

The job of the sales manager is to make sure that the sales person is in a driven, goal-oriented mental state and as motivated as he can be.

It is always a numbers game when it comes to sales. The more meetings a sales person has, the higher his sales result.

Your job as the sales manager is to keep the number of meetings of all your sales people as high as you can and by the law of averages you will reach a higher sales result.

Training new employees

In order to develop great sales people, the first few weeks and months are vitally important. You need to shape the mental attitude and work ethic of every new employee right from the start. If you fail to do it right, you will turn potentially great employees into below average performing people.

Leading a new sales person starts very early. It already starts in the interviewing process. You should call the person after the interview assuming someone else did the actual interview and ask him how it went. You should encourage the person and let him know that you believe in him. **The goal is to develop a strong emotional bond and relationship right from the start.**

Typically, a new employee will go through an initial training program to learn everything about the company and the business model. If he attends a seminar or internal training, make sure to communicate with him every day and find out if there are things in his motivation or understanding that need clarification. **Basically, hold his hand in the very beginning and make him feel like you really care.**

The main thing is that you as the team leader will be his most important person and you need to develop a relationship of trust. Make sure that you know exactly how he feels about everything so that you can adjust his motivation in case he is off track.

The first phase is a very unsure phase were you can lose a lot of new sales people if they are left alone with their issues or problems because they have never sold anything before. **Your job is to help them through the initial phase as closlely as possible so that the new sales person won't quit due to fear or rejection or failure.**

The job of the new employee is to set new appointments but the sales meeting should be done together with the new employee. **The team leader should make the first 10 to 20 meetings with clients together with the new sales person.** He should show by example how it is done. He should prove by example that he can close a deal and how the sales process is done.

The most important things in the first few weeks are:

1. Identification with the company and the job

- Tell him about positive examples and stories with clients that you experienced in the past
- Give him extra information about the market and industry that you are in and show him how important his job is
- Tell him how your company is taking care of clients and how poorly the competition does

2. Vision

- Give him a vision of what he can accomplish in your company
- Tell him about income opportunities
- How great the job of a sales person can be (more freedom, flexibility, time for family, money)
- Talk about future career opportunities

3. Praise and recognition

- Give him as much praise and recognition as you can even for little things
- People crave praise and typically don't get any recognition for their accomplishments in other companies

4. Fun

- Make sure to show him that it can be a lot of fun to work in your company
- Go out with the guys once in a while and make sure that not everything is about business

5. Money

- The new sales person must see and feel that people make a lot of money in this business. Therefore, you should drive an expensive car, wear nice suits, have a nice watch and carry lots of cash with you.
- Remember: Sales people are driven by money and the opportunity to make money. The goal is to show him what he can potentially have and motivate him with what is possible for him. The key is to let him understand that the sales job is a tool for him to make money and to reach all of his financial goals.

Training and educating new sales people

I personally put a lot of emphasis on training and educating my people. I rather spend an hour teaching them some knowledge than spending it with a pep talk. It is very important that the sales person feels competent about the products and the sales tools so that he has a lot of self-confidence when talking to a client.

> *Motivation alone is never enough.*

The first time a new sales person is doing cold calls, it is very important that the manager is right next to him during the first few hours. He needs to **help the sales person to get over the initial fear and to break the ice. Nothing can be more frustrating for a new sales person than to be left alone with a negative experience of making phone calls**. If that is the case, it is just a matter of time until you lose that employee.

It is your complete responsibility for the first three months to make sure that your new sales person makes any kind of sales. If he doesn't make enough appointments, you need to schedule a telephone session with him and force him to make calls.

Especially in the beginning it is vitally important that you have very high demands in the first few weeks. You need to push him so that he will be shaped to become an active sales person. You can always go back later once he is used to the high pace.

Only once he has mastered the basics like prospecting, presenting, closing, etc. is it possible for him to fully function on his own. If he is still not good enough in those areas you need to help him and be responsible for his sales result.

The best kind of leadership is always to lead by example. Either you are a great sales person yourself who closes deals like no one else or your team must dominate the sales stats. Otherwise your people will not give you the necessary respect and it is almost impossible to shape and lead them.

Dealing with demotivated sales people

Every sales person will once in while have a bad day. Meetings get cancelled, deals get reversed or clients get angry. Unfortunately, that is part of a typical sales job.

> *When someone is just starting out in this field,*
> *he will take everything too personally and his feeling get hurt*
> *very easily when he get rejected by a client.*

That is why you need to have daily contact in the first three months with your new sales person. You need to know in what emotional mood he is.

Sometimes all someone needs in a moment like this is a few encouraging words. Here are five examples:

- *"This happened to me as well when I started..."*
- *"80% of our customers love our products but 20% don't like it. Who should we try to make happy?"*
- *"50% of the money that we make is for the actual work that we have done. The other 50% is money for the pain that we had to experience."*
- *"Should one person who got angry be responsible to destroy all of your goals and dreams? I don't think so."*
- *"If one person doesn't like our services, then that's ok. There are thousands of others who are grateful for what we have to offer."*

The best way to get someone out of a negative emotional funk is to encourage him to get back on the horse right away by making new phone calls or calling up other existing clients. But it is key that you are with him in that moment and can control that situation and give him new emotional strength right then and there. Ideally, you want to achieve some little success by setting new appointments or getting a new sale. Anyway, **you will need to produce something positive so that he learns that a low doesn't mean the end.**

The four phases for leadership

Basically, there are four types of leadership styles that you can apply. In the beginning the motivation of a new sales person is generally higher but his competence is low. Over time the competence goes up and the motivation goes down.

In the **first phase** you need to have very close contact with your sales person. You give him clear instructions and check all of his activities and scheduled meetings. You teach him how the job should be done ideally and your control should be very strict.

> *If you treat people as if they were better already,*
> *they tend to try to fulfill this expectation.*

It is important that you give him lots of praise and recognition for the things that he does well. Let me give you an example: If he is making a practice sales presentation in front of you and it is horrible, then you can't destroy his motivation by telling him that it was horrible. You need to find the things that he did well and mention those first. Then he feels good about himself and is open for suggestions to improve the rest. Make sure that you teach him all the necessary psychological tools to be successful in sales.

In the **second phase** you give him a bit more freedom but you still need to make sure that he is doing the necessary amount of meetings. In this phase you need to focus on perfectioning the basic sales steps, which means lots of trainings.

In the **third phase** you need to set goals for your employee that he can reach. Your job is to find out where his weaknesses are and try to eliminate them as much as possible. Remember a sales person is only as good as his weakest link.

In the **fourth phase** your employee is independent and can reach goals on his own. The job of the manager is only to make sure that sales results are achieved and that the person is motivated.

Motivation and vision

> *A clear vision, backed by definite plans, gives you*
> *a tremendous feeling of confidence and personal power.*

According to statistics of sales organizations **new sales people tend to leave a company in the first 8 to 12 weeks of starting a new sales job.**

Typically, people leave because they are disappointed and haven't reached their targets. That is why motivation is key. Most people chose a sales job because they want to make more money, get recognition or do something more meaningful with their lives. Some people want to climb the ladder of an organization and want to become leaders themselves.

That is why you need to create personal vision together with your new sales person that goes beyond the first few weeks.

You need to create a career path with him so that he is not only motivated by money and closing deals in the short run but also by the opportunities over the next few years that the company has to offer.

There are lots of tools like incentives to go on a trip or to get a certain price but the real motivation should come from his vision of becoming a great team manager himself.

Another very strong factor is the recognition that you give him in front of others. When you do a team meeting, mention his accomplishments in front of the other team members. This will give him the motivation to repeat a positive result because we are all driven by recognition and we usually don't get enough. Napoleon also said that people will die for ribbons.

The main goal of developing a motivated sales person is to give him a vision so that he can develop a motivation on his own. **Outside motivation is important in the beginning but he will only be successful in the long run if he develops a motivation that comes from within.**

Praise and recognition

> *The only thing that people want more than money and sex is praise and recognition.*

You can never give enough praise and recognition. The general rule is to praise once too many times than not doing it enough. Most people are lacking recognition and only get a feedback when they are doing something wrong. The type of leadership is a disasterous strategy. **Use every opportunity to give praise and recognition for your employees.**

Identification with the company and the products

If someone doesn't 100% believe in the products that they are selling they will never achieve anything. They need to be convinced that they have the best products in the world otherwise they will not be able to convince other people.

You need to be able to show and prove to your people that the business that you are in is a growing and thriving business. You need to show your people the opportunities that lie in your company and in your field. Explain with facts why it makes sense to work for your company and in your industry.

Another factor to identify with the company is the general mood and level of fun that people experience in your company. **So always be in a good mood and smile a lot. It is contagious. People are only motivated to work and perform well in an environment that is positive and fun.**

Organize a team evening once a month where you go bowling, go karting, for dinner or some other fun event. Also, take the time to out for a drink after work and make sure that a few people go. It is important for team building and identification.

As a sales manager you have a higher income than your employee. Drive a nice car and wear nice clothes. Pay for dinner and don't give up a vibe that money is tight. It is the little things that people notice. If your employee believes that you are financially successful, he will believe that he can achieve the same and is therefore motivated to work harder.

How to criticize employees the right way

Nothing can be more destructive than destructive criticism. You will lose your people and the opportunity to make more money if you kill their motivation.

> ### *Never criticize anyone infront of others.*

Criticism can only take place in a closed environment and if no more than 2 sets of eyes are present. Never do it over the phone. **Do it always in person. Always make it very personal.**

The perfect way to criticize someone is to **criticize the behavior and never the person itself.** Don't ever say *"you are a loser"* or *"an idiot"* or something like that. Never attack the person. Instead say things like: *"Your behavior in this situation was unacceptable."* Or say: *"What you did to this customer was not ok."*

You should take about 30 seconds and not more for your criticism and then use another 30 seconds to build him back up immediately.

It could go something like this: *"Your behavior in this situation was unacceptable. The way you communicated with this co-worker was really inappropriate. I expect you not to talk like this ever again. You are normally such a great person with such a fantastic personality. You don't need to lower yourself to a level like that. This kind of behavior is so untypical for you, don't you think? I believe in you and I think that you have the potential for greatness in you and this behavior was not in alignment of who you really are. You are better than that."*

Another way to set standards is to communicate in the very beginning what you expect of your employees. You could give a general presentation of what is not acceptable behavior or performance. This way you set the rules right from the start and you can refer back to them if someone is out of line.

Another great way to let people know what not to do is to criticize yourself or your own behavior in front of others. By doing so, you let people know what you expect but you do it indirectly. You don't actually have to say it to them and they will not lose their face.

And a last option is to tell your people a story of a former employee and let them know how his behavior was not acceptable and how he got fired. People usually get it on their own.

No, no's

There are things that you should never do as a manager:

1. Never lend any money to an employee. You cross a personal line and you will never see it again. If he cannot perform on his own, then he is the wrong person for your organization.
2. Never complain in front of your people. Nothing will kill their motivation and identification with the company faster than a manager who is criticizing the company itself.
3. Never speak badly about others.
4. Never criticize or embarrass someone in front of others.
5. Never let an employee challenge your authority in front of others.
6. Don't fire someone in front of others. Always do it in private. If you fire someone in front of everybody you might set an example but it will create an environment of scared employees.

> *"A dead fish starts first stinking from the head."*
> (German saying)

If you lose the respect of your people because of your own behavior or your own inability to make sales, you will have soon have a rebellion on your hands. **People will not follow you if you start to doubt you.** Therefore you should never show any doubts and you need to make sure that your own behavior is always perfect and a role model. If you lose respect, it's over.

Team meetings

Team meetings are an important leadership tool to motivate your team. You could have a team meeting once a week, twice a month or once a month. Having too many team meetings can be boring for your people and I prefer doing them once a month and having a personal meeting with each employee once a week. **It is important that you don't necessarily have the new sales people in the same meeting with the older guys. Some of the older guys are usually more negative or just average performing people and they will be a bad influence on the still highly motivated new sales people.** In that case do two different meetings. Don't put them all in the same room together.

You should present new information about the company, talk about monthly sales budgets, motivate the people with earning examples and remind them of reasons why they are in the industry and chose this sales job. Teach them a sales tool each time so that they keep getting better in their sales skills.

Let the people publicly communicate their sales targets in a team meeting and make a list on a flip chart. Write down each name and their personal sales goal next to it so that everybody can see it. Make sure that they commit to their number and because they have to do it infront of everybody else, they will have to reach their targets so that they don't lose face. It can be a great motivational tool.

In my experience you should take all those numbers, add them up and take 60% of that total number to determine your team target. That is going to be a more realistic number. It is typical that people will give you a higher number and then only reach about 60% of that because of unforeseen things that will always get in the way.

The One Minute Manager Meets the Monkey

Ken Blanchard's book *"The One Minute Manager meets the Monkey"* was a turning point in my career as a team manager. When a person goes to the boss with a problem and the boss agrees to do something about it, the monkey is off his back and onto the boss's. The book is about a story of a manager who is overworked, overwhelmed and constantly stressed by the workload. When his employees come to him with a problem, he takes on their tasks and his workload is even higher. Basically, he took on their monkey. Monkies are not projects or problems but always the next step of what needs to be done.

In order to free yourself as a manager from all the little tasks that your employees ask of you, you need to give them back their monkies and let them do the work themselves. This way you will make them more independent and you will have more time to deal with the things that are important to you.

Let me give you an example: An employee comes to you with a problem or a task. Instead of taking on that problem, you will ask the employee the following things:
1. **What do you think needs to be done first?**
2. **How do you solve this problem by yourself?**
3. **What would you do?**

Then you listen to his answer and if necessary you will give him additional instructions on how to best deal with the problem.

But you don't do it for him. It is vitally important that he will try to solve the problem on his own with your instructions. If you fail to do this you will always have people who are never independent and you will constantly expect you to solve their problems and tasks. Even if you could do it much faster and quicker, you will become their slave.

The last step is to make sure that he will report back to you confirming that the issue has been resolved or come back to you with additional questions so that he can try it again. By giving back the monkey you will free yourself from unnecessary jobs that an employee should be performing. It is a form of delegation with control but without your direct involvement.

Personal talks and goal setting for employees

If the plan doesn't work, then change then plan, not the goal.

A personal talk with an employee is an important job that you should do at least once a week for about one hour with each sales person. You should start the conversation very friendly and positive with lots of small talk and personal questions about his life, his family or his hobbies. Praise him for good sales results or for things that he has done well. The first five minutes are always focused on creating a positive mood and trying to feel where the other person is emotionally.

The main part of the personal talk should be dynamic and motivating. Prepare yourself well in advance and set goals with your employee. Make sure that you check whether he is on track each time you talk to him. Depending on the personality structure of your employee your conversation style will vary. Some will need more facts, others more motivation.

The goal of every sales manager is to motivate or enable his people to create more results. If you set a goal with an employee of reaching a sales target of $10,000 in commission but you know that he is only capable of reaching half of that, then you must identify a way of helping him to close that gap. Ask yourself in which areas does he need to be more skillful? What kind of knowledge is he missing? What can you actively do to help him achieve his goal? Make an analysis of his current situation and try to identify solutions of how to reach his goals.

Sometimes people are at their wits end and have no sales and no money. In a situation like this there is really only one solution. You need to address his failure from an emotional place. **You need to realize that it was your responsibility that the employee is where he is at right now.**

You either failed to force him to set enough meetings, to train him properly, to motivate him properly or to let him go when you should have done it earlier. But at this point where everything seems to be bad, your options are limited. You need to decide whether you want to keep him and fight for him or if you will let him go.

This is how you can emotionally challenge him:

"I know that you have no more money today. I know that you feel that there is nothing that you can do right now. But now imagine for a moment that something terrible happened. Imagine that your mother is sick and that there is only one kind of operation that could save her. But this operation will cost $50,000. Imagine that if you don't come up with the $50,000 by closing 20 new clients that your mother will die in 14 days. Would you be able to do it? Yes. Would you be able to save her life? Yes. What would you do? (Ask anyone, work like crazy, call the whole world, etc.) Exactly. So you are telling me that in an extreme situation like that you would be able to do it? Yes. Luckily, we don't have a situation like that and I hope your mother will live to be 100 years old. But looking at your current financial situation and lack of sales, don't you think that you are in a similar place? Isn't this also an emergency? So do it."

Analysis of your employee - what can he do well and where's he weak?

If an employee is not reaching his sales targets than it is always one of two reasons: He is simply not good enough in the basic sales elements like prospecting, presenting, closing, etc. (not technical or product knowledge) or his mental attitude is wrong.

I have found that most people want to be successful but they are not able because of lack of training in the basic sales elements. **Check the basic sales elements:**

- Asking for referrals
- Setting enough first meetings
- Pre-Sales Techniques
- Closing rate
- Receiving referrals
- Sales consultation and selling techniques
- Other factors

- Prospecting on the phone
- Presentation
- Time frame of a meeting (too long or too short)
- Proper analysis of the data from the meeting

Ask your employee to give himself a number from 1 to 10 in each area – 1 being the lowest level of skill and expertise and 10 being the highest. **Most people don't want to judge themselves too low generally speaking so make sure you check the areas where he scores himself average.** Mostly that is where the main problems are. Don't procrastinate with his training and don't hope that he will figure it out on his own. Sooner or later he will fail because of a weakness in one those areas. Really analyze and ask about details in each area until you find out where the problem for his lack of sales is.

> *You will only be able to make positive changes*
> *if you really know what the problem is.*

Sometimes we like a person so much and we believe so much in his future potential that we forget that he is still a rookie and learning the basic sales elements. You need to make sure to teach each one of your people so well that they become great communicators and that they do the things that work. Don't hope but take charge.

Personal development for a leader

You should always know more that your people. You also need to work on your own skills and knowledge to become better. You should study and read everything about your industry. You should go to seminars and learn new skills and techniques. You should read books about sales, marketing, business and leadership. **You need to make sure that your people will not get better over time and you stood still in your own personal development. If that is the case you will lose the respect of your people.**

I personally would suggest listening to audio programs of Brian Tracy and other successful business coaches. Brian has definitely made a positive impact on my career and personal development. Make it your own commitment to constantly learn, read or listen to audio programs. The more positive things you will feed your mind the better and more positive will you become.

The best books about business and success

I have put together a list of the books that I recommend for every sales person or sales manager to read. These books have had a huge impact in my own life and I have gifted those books to each of my sales people after they have reached a certain level. Invest into your people. It will be worth it.

The top three books for your sales people are:

1. How to win friends and influence people *(Dale Carnegie)*
2. Think and grow rich *(Napoleon Hill)*
3. How I raised myself from failure to success in selling *(Frank Bettger)*

Other great books about business, successs and leadership and life:

1. The One Minute Manager Series *(Kenneth Blanchard)*
2. Thinking Big *(Brian Tracy)*
3. Start Small, Finish Big *(Fred De Luca)*
4. Unlimited Selling Power *(Moine)*
5. Unlimited Power *(Anthony Robbins)*
6. Rich Dad, Poor Dad *(Robert Kiyosaki)*
7. Beyond Selling *(Dan S. Bagley)*
8. Multiple Streams of Income *(Robert G. Allen)*
9. The E-Myth Revisited *(Michael E. Gerber)*
10. Cashflow Quadrant *(Robert Kiyosaki)*
11. Pour Your Heart into it *(Howard Schultz)*
12. Men are from mars, women are from venus *(John Gray)*

This is just a small selection of some of the books that I have read and that I recommend.

Lead different employees differently (red, green, blue, yellow)

There are four different personality types: red, blue, green and yellow type. Each one of them describes the most common character traits of that type. Some people are more extroverted and loud and others – this would be the red type. Others are numbers oriented and like computers – this would be the blue type. And then there are people who are very social and friendly like predominantly the green type. The yellow type is very unconventional just to give you an example.

There is no good or bad personality structure. Every personality structure has strengths and weaknesses. Most people have a dominant type and a secondary type. Based on the type that someone is you can find out what comes easier to that person and what doesn't.

• Red type
Impulsive, dominate, engaged, impatient, emotional, loud, active, dynamic, courageous, conflict ready, goal-oriented, prepared to take risks, will-strong, likes confrontation and challenges, demanding, restless, direct, likes adventure, alive, no patience
Typical occupations: sales person, pioneer, leadership role
Sports: like race car driver, fighter, bungee jumping, individual sports

• Blue type
Detail-oriented, precise, organized, systematic, steady, patient, reasonable, makes lots of plans, principle-faithfully, introverted, avoids physical contact, ironic, feelings are hardly recognizable, isolated, quiet, serious, on time, good with finances
Typical occupations: Tax counsel, programmer, accountant, Computer specialist
Sports: Persistent kinds of sport, moving, running, chess

• Green type
Talkative, friendly, kind, makes others feel comfortable, ready to compromise, accommodating, likes to tell stories about the past, social, reassuring, open-hearted, emotional
Typical occupations: social worker, kindergarten teacher, customer service
Sports: Team player

• Yellow type

Innovative, artistic, communicative, unorthodox, versatile, spontaneous, flexible, surprising, tolerant, inspiring, superficial, influential, creative

Typical occupations: Artist, publicity man, speaker, creative occupations

Sports: Mental games and exercises

Depending on the personality of your employee you need to focus more on his type if you want to get through to him and build trust. The same is true for dealing with clients.

> ## *If you want to motivate someone you need to understand how they are wired.*

If you know how or with which tool you can motivate them, you will get further ahead.

When talking to the red type you need to talk to him in a dynamic manner. You can motivate the red type with money, recognition, status and power. You can even challenge him or make compete against him (with achieveing sales results). You can motivate him with things or prices.

When it comes to the blue type you need to give him information, facts, statistics and numbers. You should analyze the numbers together with him and based on that develop a strategy. This will be his main motivation.

When dealing with the green type you need to focus on the relationship. You need to be nice, friendly and talk about past stories. Make sure you praise him for great customer service and show him that you are his friend.

The yellow type wants to be special and different from anybody else. You can inspire him with reaching a special status within the firm or a special position that no one else has. Let him be creative in his approach.

Emotional intelligence and relationship management

The most important quality of a good manager is his ability to develop relationships with his people. **The level of his emotional intelligence is much more important than the level of his intellectual intelligence.**

A leader must be able to "feel" how a person is doing and then be able to use his interpersonal relationship skills to steer him in the right direction. A leader must be compassionate and understanding and his people need to be very close to him emotionally. **People will not follow a person who is a tyrant. People will follow a leader who there for them when they need him.** People will achieve great results because they don't want to disappoint their manager. It is seldom the money why they are selling. It is the recognition that they will get from their manager why they will perform well.

People say that you shouldn't mix friendship with business. I don't think that is always true. Especially when it comes to sales organizations. A sales organization can be a place where you get the emotional support from your friends and co-workers. **It is the manager's job to create an environment where people feel appreciated and that is fun.** The manager needs to organize events that are outside of the business to develop a strong sense of team building. The stronger the team, the better the sales results.

Qualities of leaders

The main qualities of a good leader are to develop a vision, to encourage his people, to lead by example and to produce results. There are four areas where a manager needs to have special characteristics: Personal, Business, Communication and Relationship.

• Personal Characteristics

There are items that can help you improve yourself, and enhance your interactions with others. Desirable personal characteristics make a manager someone that others can look up to, and feel comfortable following:

1. Self-Motivation:

An effective manager can't motivate others if he or she can't self-motivate. Self-motivation, the ability to get yourself going, and take charge of what's next for you, is a vital personal characteristic for a manager. You have to keep yourself going and motivate those who work with you.

2. Integrity:

People trust a good manager because they know he or she has personal integrity. Workers need to know that you will fight for them, do what you say, and follow the rules.

3. Dependability/Reliability:

As a person, you should be dependable and reliable. Your superiors, as well as your subordinates, need to know that you can be counted on. Others in the organization should be able to rely on you.

4. Optimism:

Do you look to the future with hope? An optimistic attitude can help build morale in your employees. Your positive attitude can inspire others, and help them feel good about getting things done.

5. Confidence:

Do you have confidence in yourself. You need to be able to make decisions in confidence, and show others that you are capable of making good decisions. Your confidence will rub off on others.

6. Calmness:

As the manager, you can't afford to break down when the pressure is on. The ability to remain calm and do what needs to be done is essential in a good manager.

7. Flexibility:

A manager needs a certain amount of flexibility, since he or she may need to adapt to changing situations.

• Business Characteristics

Some level of business knowledge and skills are important when you are a manager.

1. Industry Knowledge:

What do you know about the industry you are in? It helps understand your industry so that you can answer questions and perform your work more effectively. Workers may not need industry knowledge, but a manager should have some.

2. Delegatation:

An effective manager knows that some tasks need to be delegated. You should be able to identify workers who will do well, and give them tasks they can succeed at while helping the project.

3. Organization:

You need to be organized in order to be a good manager. Keep track of projects, employees and assignments so that you are on top of what needs to happen in the business.

4. Financial Management:

Understand basic financial concepts so that you understand how to manage money as part of a project you have been given.

5. Legal Implications:

While you don't need to be a law expert, you should have a grasp of the legal implications of sexual harassment, proper hiring and firing practices, confidentiality, and more.

• Communication Qualities

A good manager needs to be able to communicate effectively. Make sure that you develop the ability to communicate as part of your job as an effective management member.

1. Written Communication:

Learn how to communicate effectively in writing. A good manager should be able to write professionally and with correct grammar, expressing him or herself in email, memos, and thank you notes.

2. Public Speaking:

As a good manager, you should know how to speak publicly, annunciating your words, and concisely communicating your ideas, whether in an interview, or addressing workers.

3. Constructive Feedback:

Learn how to provide feedback in a way that is helpful to workers and others.

4. Active Listening:

One of the most important communication skills is listening. Make sure you are listening to your workers, superiors and customers, and that you acknowledge them.

5. Presentations:

Organize and practice your presentations before giving them so that you are clear and concise, and so that your presentation flows well.

• Relationship Qualities

Your characteristics as you build relationships matter when you are a manager. You will need to know how to manage relationships between yourself and your subordinates, as well as manage the relationships among those who work under you.

1. Customer Service:

You might be surprised to discover the customer service is a relationship quality. You need to be able to build good relationships with customers if you want to be a good manager. Learn how to relate to customers, and see things from their perspective.

2. Mediator:

Do you know how to make peace? Often, a good manager needs to be able to act as a mediator between workers, between a worker and a client, or between a superior and a worker. Brush up on your mediation qualities, and learn conflict resolution techniques to be a good manager.

3. Team Player:

Are you part of a team? You need to be able to function as part of a team if you want to succeed as an effective manager. Make sure that you are willing to work with others, and that you will hold up your end.

4. Respect:

You need to be respectful of your workers if you are to have respect as a manager in return. It's up to you to set the example and build relationships of respect.

5. Collaboration:

You'll need to set up collaborations with others, and with your team. You should also be able to work well with others, and understand how to integrate ideas and personalities.

6. Value Others:

A good manager helps employees feel valued. Surveys show that employees want recognition from their superiors, and you need to make sure to recognize contributions from your workers.

Hiring and firing people

Hiring the right kind of people for your company can make all the difference. **The better your people, the better your company.** Therefore you need to make sure that you hire the right kind of people.

Depending on the job there are different personality qualities that people need to have in order to perform well. Typically, you want to have a more outgoing person in sales and a well-structured and organized person for an administrational job. That is why I always do a personality test as a part of the hiring process.

> *A personality test can give you a good indication whether the person is suited for the job.*

Also, I recommend doing at least two different interviews with two different people to have two opinions. You should also let the person wait in the waiting room and ask the secretary afterward how the person behaved and what kind of vibe she got from him. Women are often a much better judge of character than men.

> ## *Get rid of negative employees the same day and without delay.*

If you need to fire an employee, do it like this: *"You did good work but I believe that you would be happier in a different company."* **Always try to have a positive conversation with someone that you must fire.**

Most of the time people will know on their own when it is time to go. **Don't delay it unnecessarily into the future. People who tend to start to become negative will influence others negatively.**

Sometimes you need to rid your organization of a high producing person because of his personality and negative influence on others. **By eliminating a person who gives off a negative vibe or mood, you will do everybody a favor and the organization will do much better overall.**

Your time is extremely valuable

Make sure that you communicate well from the start that your time is very valuable and that you don't waste it on unimportant issues. Some employees can be very time consuming and hinder the manager of effectively doing his job.

You decide how much time how much time you allocate to each person and not the other way around. You are not the service man for everybody who is supposed to be available on call. You need to make sure that you reach your goals and if an employee needs more time or energy, you must decide whether it is worth it.

Your time management skills become even more important when you are a manager. **Sometimes things can be urgent but you don't need to be on call for everybody at all times. They can leave a message with your assistant** while you have your day planned and you check on her a couple times a day to see if there is something really pressing and important. After all your important tasks are done you make your calls at the end of the day with your people.

> *Nothing is so urgent that it cannot wait 24 hours.*

If everything depends on you in urgent matters then you need to change something in your business approach. You need to initiate things and not react to things that are happening around you. Remember there are four tasks groups:

1. Things are important and urgent
2. Things are important but not urgent
3. Things are not important but urgent
4. Things are not important and not urgent

Focus your time and energy only on the first two points.

Getting an assistant

Get an assistant for your weaknesses and administrational work. Don't try to do everything on your own. **Delegate everything except for financial matters and things that cannot be delegated. Don't lose time with little unimportant things like administration that can be done by someone else.**

Also, if you are a manager and you are making good money, you don't need to do your household cleaning anymore. The five hours that it takes you each week for cleaning, ironing or laundry can be spent more wisely in your job.

If you pay a cleaning lady $10 per hour and she comes once a week, you will spend $50 per week. If you are in sales and you make a commission of $1000 per deal that you close, you should simply use those five hours to close one more deal.

A good manager is a master in delegation. But be careful: you need to make a list of what you delegate. You need to check after a couple of days if the task really has been done. Don't just assume. You can also tell your assistant to let you know in two days if the task has been completed or if she needs further instructions. Make sure you get that feedback.

Start your career today!

Being a manager can be stressful at times but being able to see how people develop and become great sales people can be a very fulfilling experience. **Become a leader that others want to follow.**

In this book I have summarized the most important lessons that I have learned during my 20-year career as a manager and leader. I hope that you can learn and apply some of the lessons from this book.

The world needs people like you who can step up and change the world. I wish you all the best and hope that you will become a great leader!

About the author

Prior to founding Norman Meier International, Norman was the Chief Executive Officer and main shareholder of a publicly listed company with a market capitalization of over $300 million.

As a successful businessman and entrepreneur he has accomplished success that many people only dream about. He built companies and financed them with millions of dollars and as a former stockbroker he has built more than 3000 clients, raised over $400 million from the private sector and $600 million from institutional clients.

Norman Meier was born and raised in Switzerland and moved to America to fulfill his personal dream. Norman has traveled and worked in many countries all over the world and speaks five languages.

He has had successful careers in sales, marketing, finance and management consulting.

Norman Meier has produced many audio and video learning programs on the topics of business, financial independence, sales and marketing and personal development. He has written and produced several audio and video learning programs and published 12 books to date.

Norman Meier has been an investment professional since 1995 and is an expert in Private Equity. He has held executive positions with top-tier global investment firms such as MAN Investments and AWD in Switzerland, and Canaccord Capital Corporation in Canada.

Norman Meier is highly educated. He has a BBA, MBA and Ph D in Human Behavior from Newport University and 12 different finance diplomas, designations and was licensed as a financial advisor in several countries.

Norman Meier was the manager of a FINRA licensed broker dealer in USA and CEO and president of a two public mining exploration companies. He was the founder and major shareholder of several gold and uranium exploration companies in the US and major shareholder of three sales organizations in Europe.

He built up a global team of over 60 employees in Switzerland, USA, Canada and Mexico. He was the president and founder of a Swiss financial services company with a license from a self-regulatory organization and a license from the Swiss Banking Commission.

Norman Meier is happily married and has four children. Besides spending time with his family, he likes working out, tennis, ice hockey, chess and he has a love for animals in need.

Printed in the United States
By Bookmasters